A Well-Designed Business®

— THE POWER TALK FRIDAY EXPERTS —

LUANN NIGARA

Published by Best Seller Publishing®, Pasadena, CA
Best Seller Publishing® is a registered trademark
Printed in the United States of America.
ISBN 978-1-092291-22-4

This publication is designed to provide accurate and authoritative information with regard to the subject matter covered. It is sold with the understanding that the publisher is not engaged in rendering legal, accounting, or other professional advice. If legal advice or other expert assistance is required, the services of a competent professional should be sought. The opinions expressed by the authors in this book are not endorsed by Best Seller Publishing® and are the sole responsibility of the author rendering the opinion.

Most Best Seller Publishing® titles are available at special quantity discounts for bulk purchases for sales promotions, premiums, fundraising, and educational use. Special versions or book excerpts can also be created to fit specific needs.

For more information, please write:
Best Seller Publishing®
1346 Walnut Street, #205
Pasadena, CA 91106
or call 1(626) 765 9750
Toll Free: 1(844) 850-3500
Visit us online at: www.BestSellerPublishing.org

Recognition & Applause

Front Cover Photo: Power Portraits™. Irina Leoni

I feel that I was born to take photos of entrepreneurs. The sparkle in an entrepreneur's eye is different than that of any other people.

The energy. The passion. The hustle. The grit. The unwavering determination. The seemingly crazy belief that they can change the world in their own unique way.

Power-Portraits.com

Front & Back Cover Layout and Creation: Curio Electro. Nicole Heymer

Are you ready to bring your brand to a wider audience? We have a plan. We can help define your voice, uncover what makes your brand memorable, and unlock new ways to bring your services to the clients searching for exactly what you do.

Curioelectro.com

Green Velvet Chair on Cover: Article.com

Our most popular sofa, reimagined as a large, cozy lounge chair. This modern take on a mid-century classic features clean lines, a tufted seat, and a luxuriously stuffed back cushion. Two matching round bolsters complete the look. And it is available in #podcastgreen!

Welldesigned.article.com

Praise on Amazon for LuAnn's First Book, *The Making of A Well-Designed Business*®

5.0 out of 5 stars - If you give a designer this book, she's gonna love to read it.
By JCerutti on March 4, 2018
    Format: Paperback Verified Purchase

I've been a fan of LuAnn's podcast for some time, listening on road trips. I've even invented a road trip or two just to listen. Her guests are always full of practical and actionable advice and LuAnn is a skilled and engaging interviewer. Since I'm driving as I listen and unable to take notes, a lot of the wisdom is lost as I get where I'm going and drawn into more immediate demands. I was thrilled when she wrote a book - hopeful that the wisdom would be written down for me. I just finished the book in one sitting and find it to be so much more than I had hoped for. I've been a designer for years, but after a major relocation and ongoing home renovation during the past 2 years, I've been on the fence about restarting in my new location. Technology and information overload is raising my i verwhelm to new heights. But here in The Making of A Well-Designed Business, I see a manual for actually getting down to it and getting some thing done. So much practical information in a logical step by step format, filled with encouragement and common-sense examples and exercises, that I feel reenergized and empowered to reinvent my business in my new location. Some lessons I learned from listening to the podcasts were reinforced in the book, and anybody who can reference "If You Give A Mouse A Cookie" in a business manual is my kind of mogul, but what struck me most is the authenticity and integrity that LuAnn lives by. You can't fake that and it's what makes her the engaging and successful powerhouse that she is.

5.0 out of 5 stars - A Treasure Trove of Knowledge!

By Reena Venkatesh on March 5, 2019
Format: Paperback Verified Purchase

What an insightful book. It's is filled with first hand experiences and LuAnn has so distinctly personalized it that as a professional in the industry reading the book I feel every word connects with me. I reach out for the book daily and read parts of it and feel it is been food for my thoughts for my business improvement on a daily basis.

Additionally I want to give a big or huge shoutout to her for her podcasts and the immense value she is bringing through them. These podcasts are a treasure trove and she is bringing to the surface, true & tried, knowledge in the interior design industry that anyone in the industry can use and learn from.

5.0 out of 5 stars - A MUST READ

By Victoria Morgan on September 13, 2018
Verified Purchase

I'm sure this book is helpful to entrepreneur at any stage, but as a new designer this has been a wealth a of knowledge I'll implement today! I'm beyond blessed to have found your podcast and now this book provides the tools I need for success. LuAnn, thank you for your diligence in sharing methods and practices that have helped you gain success. I am, much like many others, eternally grateful for your willingness to share, teach and motivate!

5.0 out of 5 stars - easy to understand
By Elizabeth A. Dreyfus on May 17, 2018
Format: Paperback Verified Purchase

Every person wishing to start a business should read this book first and do what it suggests. Had this been available back when I was starting different businesses, I think I would not have made some frustrating and expensive mistakes. At this time I am starting up a non-profit and this book is a textbook of what should be done. We are following it extensively. So far, we have not been "lucky"—we have been successful.

"The Making of a Well-Designed Business" is a comprehensive, easy to understand, a quick read and even has humor.

5.0 out of 5 stars - This is a great book! A MUST read that defines the basics …
By John Arnett on May 12, 2018
Format: Paperback Verified Purchase

This is a great book! A MUST read that defines the basics of a well-designed business. Easy to read and understand. Includes some great stories, lessons learned and practical tips to help you brainstorm, dream and focus. My opinion...great for any endeavor you may be pursuing as I direct a small non-profit with an international reach. Fantastic job, LuAnn Nigara!

Gratitude

We are each the sum of everyone who has touched our lives, of every experience we have had, and of every road taken and not taken.

Our businesses are the same. They, too, are the sum of everyone who has mentored us, who has taught us, who has held our hand when it was hard, and who has raised their hand when it was time to celebrate.

Today I thank those who have helped me and touched me in my business journey.

It begins with my husband Vin. Everything always begins and ends with him. He and I are so fortunate to truly share a special love. We both recognize it and we are both consciously thankful for it. In addition to this, he has been the single greatest business mentor I could have ever conjured up. He is smart, he sees potential, he teaches, he encourages, and he puts the brakes on when it is necessary. It is my great privilege to be by his side in life and in business.

Our business partner, Bill Campesi. Without his technical skill, his artistic skill, his ability to solve problems, and his caring and patient handling of our clients and our installation team, all the business savvy in the world couldn't have created what Window Works has become. Bill is the secret sauce to Window Works.

My coauthors. Each and every one of these people have blown my mind with their expertise, their ability to impart that expertise, and their passion for teaching us how to be better businesspeople. Both the podcast and Window Works have benefitted from their lessons and strategies on how to run a profitable business. I am so proud to have them with me in this book.

My extended team, who makes it all happen.

Our Window Works crew, our installers and salespeople, but especially Kimberly Serafim and Adriana Stapelman. These ladies are often called on to help with podcast duties in addition to their regular work. They are always happy to lend a hand, and I appreciate it.

Christie Rocha, my daughter and my right hand in all things podcast. She manages all the details, juggles more balls than you can imagine, fields dozens of messages from me in a day, coming by email, Voxer, text, and phone call. Miraculously she handles it all with a calm and steady resolve.

Regina Somerruk, my mom, who listens to every single show.

Team Podcast. Christy Haussler is a lifesaver, period. Schedule changes, last minute uploads, and so on are always handled with patience and humor.

Curio Electro. Nicole Heymer is exceptionally skilled and remarkably detailed in all things website, branding, graphic design, and most importantly, keeping me on point.

Samson Media. Gene Sower and his team took us from ground up in email list set up, newsletter creation, and social media posting. It would not have been possible without your expertise.

Room Two Productions, my sound editors. Your level of excellence and your attention to detail are remarkable. You'll never really know how much your commitment to me and to this show are so deeply valued and appreciated.

Our featured sponsors, Kravet Inc. and Mydoma Studio. Your commitment to helping designers run a profitable business and your belief that it is possible are evident. I am grateful for your support in helping me help every designer create a well-designed business.

You, the podcast listener and the podcast guest. Your willingness to share your triumphs as well as your struggles with me, whether it was on the podcast, in an email, or through a social media post have taught me valuable lessons and have made me a better business owner. It is your drive for success, and your hunger for information that reminds me and inspires me to always bring my A-Game.

My sincere thank you to every one of you.

Co-Authors

NICOLE HEYMER

PETER LANG

MICHELE WILLIAMS

NANCY GANZEKAUFER

SARAH DANIELE

CLAIRE JEFFORD

EILEEN HAHN

FRED BERNS

MARC MCDONOUGH

SHAUNA LYNN SIMON

KAE WHITAKER

STACEY BROWN RANDALL

Contents

Introduction

By LuAnn Nigara

After nearly four decades and over three years of podcasting, working with and talking with interior designers just like you, I know what you struggle with. You love to design, and you hate the business side. It's not a news flash. We're all the same way. It's like loving cookies and hating being chubby. We want the good stuff without the bad stuff. I get it, and I'm with you.

Invoicing, asking for money, resolving conflicts over unmet expectations, constantly wondering where and when the next client will show up, struggling to get to the next level with the clients who actually have a decent budget, spending hours a week with social media, and wondering if it is effective. I know, I have heard you, and I want to help you.

I know you dream about having an interior design firm that runs like a ship where all the projects are well managed, your employees are happy and productive, your bills are paid, your bank account is full, and your creative juices are always flowing and on fire. Yup, I know.

You can have that. Yes, you can. And it starts today. If you read my first book, *The Making of A Well-Designed Business®*, then you know in that book I shared with you the magic pill for being a successful entrepreneur. Yes, I did, right there in the introduction. I didn't even make you read the whole book to get to it. I'm going to spill it again here. The secret to success in business, in anything, in everything, the magic pill, is you. It is your decision to recognize that you are in charge of your business, and you are responsible for its success or failure. It is not the economy, it is not the area of the country you live in, it is not the clientele; it is fully, 100 percent you. While this can be a bit intimidating, maybe even a little scary, isn't it really the best news ever? Isn't it just fantastic to know that if you are the magic pill for success, then you certainly must be in the driver's seat? You are the one person who can make the difference in your business so you can be profitable and successful.

Of course it is.

All you have to do is decide to run your business with intention, utilize the best tools available to you, and practice sound strategies that can be duplicated and repeated every day ensuring successful outcomes.

I mean, that's all…

Maybe it is just a tiny bit harder to do than it is to say. The truth is that if it were so easy to do, everyone would be successful, wouldn't they?

What about you? What decision will you make? Will you be the business owner who takes the responsibility, looks in the mirror, and says, "That's it. Today I turn this ship around. Today I chart a new course for myself, my business, and my future. Today I decide I am worthy and capable of being both creative and profitable."

Alright, let's do it. Let's make it happen. Here's how.

The podcast is a great start. Through the podcast, you often learn things you didn't know you needed to know when it comes to running an interior design firm and that can be eye opening in an "uh-oh" kind of way. However, with the podcast, you also get hope, inspiration, and motivation that it can be done, because others have done it before you. This book is a terrific next step because, together with my esteemed coauthors, we are going to lay out twelve areas of your interior design business that if you address and gain control over, you will achieve the results you desire.

Mastery is not expected in every area. We all have strengths and weaknesses as people, as business owners, and as designers. However, if you want to do more than simply exist in business, if you want to thrive and be profitable, you need to have, at minimum, competency in the important areas of running your business or you need to hire competency. Sometimes you even need to hire mastery for a gap in your skillset.

In this book, we provide you with the road map for these critical areas of running your interior design business: Defining Your Brand; Setting up Systems and Processes; What to Expect from Your CPA; How to Plan for Profit; How to Charge What You Are Worth; Managing Client Expectations; Leveraging Referrals; Instagram Strategies; Email Marketing Strategies; Marketing to Attract Luxury Clients; How to Create Exceptional Employees; and Business Principles of Home Staging.

As I say on the podcast, it's straight talk and it's action. Are you ready? Let's get started!

Section One

The Foundation for Success

CHAPTER 1

Nicole Heymer

Nicole Heymer was introduced to me by my dear friend and colleague, Sandra Funk, the principal of House of Funk. One night at Sandra's "The Attitude Is Gratitude" party, a yearly party she throws for her clients and colleagues, Sandra turned to me and said, "Lu, you have to meet Nicole. She is brilliant, and you definitely are going to want to have her on your show".

The rest, as they say, is history.

Since then, Nicole has been on my show twice, on episodes #125 and #317; she has built both my windowworks-nj.com website and my luannnigara.com website; and she has become a trusted part of my team in all things imaging, messaging, and branding. In any given month, we have a dozen conversations, and she always tells it like it is, which I just love. But it is more than that. Nicole has a radar for seeing the forest within the trees whenever I'm in a quandary about a concept or debating a direction. You know how you can walk into Home Goods and pick out that perfect piece in the middle of all the things that look like tag sale items? Nicole does that with branding. She knows the difference between a silly idea and a clever idea, the difference between a wishy-washy message and a direct call-to-action message.

As you read Nicole's chapter, take what she shares to heart. I realize branding can sometimes feel like a lofty concept or an elusive notion. If you know that feeling and you have any fuzziness around your brand, really sit

with her advice and her strategies, follow her common-sense approach, and you will gain clarity. When you know who you are, and you can express it, it is the truest calling card for attracting your ideal client.
   - LN

Defining Your Brand, Crafting Your Reputation
By Nicole Heymer

What if you assessed fifty interior design businesses based on their online presence alone?

Odds are, you wouldn't remember most of them. It's like visiting Rome: the first chapel you see is astonishing. The second is amazing, too. By the time you've seen the fifth, you're experiencing art overload and even the most ridiculously impressive Renaissance masterpieces start to blend together.

But what if you knew the story behind them? Maybe the artist who painted that section of the ceiling was eight years old, or the scene depicted was controversial, or a message in the carvings had supposedly changed people's lives? Messaging and storytelling make all the difference. Without them, even the most beautiful things can become a real snooze.

So it is with many interior design brands.

The problem is certainly not a lack of beauty, skill, or functionality. It's a lack of narrative. It's a lack of branding and a lack of messaging.

What exactly is branding?

Is it some airy concept that includes phrases like "cohesive synergy" and "proportion of vision"? Nope. Good branding is concrete, actionable, and useful. *Great* branding leads to more clients, a better experience for your clients, and a better experience for you as a business owner. The process of branding is a practical one. It will help you.

Just so we're clear: You will find a LOT of definitions for branding out there. Some will exhaust you with overcomplicated business jargon, so let's keep this really straightforward and easy to remember.

Your brand is what you are known for. It is your reputation as a business. Quite simply, it's how people think of and describe you: "Oh, yes! That's the interior design firm that _____." What comes to mind when someone thinks about your business? That's your brand.

When building your brand, you want to be the one defining the first thoughts that spring into the minds of your audience. There are three key components to help you drive the narrative:

1. Visual Branding: What you see. The visuals that allow a person to recognize your brand quickly. This can include the logo design, fonts, color palette, style of photography, patterns, shapes, and icons, among other elements.
2. Brand Voice: This is not what you say, but how you say it. What does the voice of your brand sound like? Is it friendly? Sarcastic? Funny? Aspirational? Do you avoid industry jargon or "implement impactful buzzwords to ensure synergistic solutionizing"? Does everything written or said by your brand feel consistent in tone? Trustworthy?
3. Messaging: This is the big one, the narrative about your brand that you choose to put into the world. It's the collection of information that you want both existing and potential clients to understand and believe.

In this chapter, we will focus on messaging—why you need it, how to figure it out, and what to do with it once you do.

Why should you care about messaging?

The right messaging is pure gold. It is the foundation of good marketing. It strengthens relationships with clients. It creates a bond with those who barely know you, and it elevates your business.

But what does this mean in practical terms? How will it help you on a typical Monday morning?

Messaging helps people want to buy your services.

Imagine that you're a consumer and you're looking for an interior designer. In this story, you have just moved to a new area, and you don't have any contacts for a referral. Or maybe you've lived in the area forever, but two different friends have recommended two different designers and you're comparing them. Let's assume that both interior design firms have beautiful work on their website and on social media, which is—let's face it—a likely scenario.

But this story has a plot twist. It looks like the first design firm is known for great service and for being extremely responsive. They discuss it on their home page and as part of their mission statement, they have testimonials that rave about the experience of working with them, and they have blog posts that include stories that allude to it. Also, they have pretty pictures.

The other design firm has somewhat generic copy ("we'll transform your space") and relies almost entirely on their photos. It's hard to tell what they stand for, other than providing the things that most interior designers provide.

If great service and responsive communication are important to you, who are you going to call first? What if you've dealt with vendors in the past who were not responsive, and you didn't exactly love it? Even if the fee is a little higher for the first design firm, if all other things are equal, which option would be more appealing to you?

Messaging makes it easier for the target client to choose you over another design firm.

Messaging makes your life easier.

Raise your hand if you've struggled with questions such as, "What should we put on our website home page, other than photos of our work?" Messaging can provide answers to a huge array of questions: What should we post on social media? How should we *caption* our social media images? How should we onboard clients? What on earth should we write about on our blog?

The answer is … (whispery ghost voice) … in the messaging.

It's difficult to shape the communication that you're putting out into the world if you don't know what you're trying to say. When you have messaging points in your back pocket, you never have to start with a blank sheet of paper. Your communication becomes cohesive and your brand starts to take shape in the minds of your potential, current, and past clients.

Messaging nurtures relationships with current clients.

Let's imagine another scenario: You're in the middle of a project and something goes wrong. (What? But everything in interior design projects always goes perfectly!) The construction team unearthed a terrifying nest of possums living within the floorboards. The kitchen is now three days off schedule, and the client is going to be less than delighted by this news.

In scenario #1, this client came in through referral or found you through Google search. But you don't have clear messaging. They have no idea if this is something you've dealt with before.

In scenario #2, they found you the same way—but you are known for something. Maybe you specialize in kitchens or, as we mentioned above, top-notch service. Perhaps you have a unique, reliable process.

In which scenario are you better equipped to handle the client? In which scenario are they already in a good mental place when it comes to your ability to manage issues as they arise? Having a defined brand is more than just marketing. It can position you in the mind of the client as an expert in your niche and a company that will provide the best possible outcomes with rock solid processes—or whatever you are best at—in place.

Solid messaging inspires trust. It is a useful tool for all involved as you ride the emotional rollercoaster of an interior design project. It says, "Hey! Don't worry. You hired someone who is known for _____."

Messaging makes referrals easier and ensures the right people are finding you.

No matter how effective your online marketing becomes, a good chunk of leads will always come in through referrals. How can you make the process easier and the leads that come in more qualified? The answer is messaging. If a former or current client has absorbed the messaging and knows exactly what to say and precisely what you're known for, your referrals will simply be better.

A lack of messaging is risky business. It puts the reputation of your company completely into the hands of other people. Instead of putting a consistent narrative out into the world, you are allowing them to write the narrative for you. Sure, a client who is recommending you will have nice things to say (thank you for that!), but you're asking them to do all of the work.

What aspects of your business do you want highlighted? What kind of projects do you actually want? What information do you want inserted into a potential client's head before they speak with you? Messaging gives a current client everything they need to refer you to the perfect future client.

Messaging creates consistency with employees and contractors.

When it comes to your business, how many tiny decisions do you make every day? When you're speaking with a client, how many on-the-spot responses do you provide to their questions? You may not have defined messaging yet, but you know—on a gut level—how you want to communicate with clients.

You know who doesn't always know that stuff? Your employees, contractors, and everyone else who isn't you. Clear messaging gives them a chance to make on-the-go decisions that are consistent with what you, as the founder, want the business to be known for.

If the goal is not to babysit those who work with you, then messaging will be helpful. It pulls the "who we are and what we do" out of your head and gets it in front of the people who help make it real.

Getting started: How do you define your messaging?

Your business is a three-dimensional creature with a personality, a history, typical behaviors, and an identifiable look. A million things make your interior design firm different (whether you realize it yet or not), but you can use messaging points to prioritize and filter them.

What is a messaging point?

A messaging point is a single idea that you want to communicate about your business. It is simple enough to be described in a sentence or a short phrase. Messaging points are for internal use, created to say what you stand for in simple, direct ways that will guide all of your communications. Some will be communicated directly, as in a tagline or in the founder's bio, and others will be demonstrated, through systems, testimonials, images, or stories.

How many messaging points should you have?

Three or four messaging points will do. Because your brand is its own unique animal, you need to communicate more than one thing. But you also want to curate this information: The goal is to provide a clear, memorable framework for people to understand what you are about and how your company, above all others, is the brand that will get them what they want.

What makes a good messaging point?

Useful, sustainable messaging isn't all about you as a business, all about being different than your competitors, or even all about the target client. It must consider everyone and everything involved. For every messaging point, we need to ask three questions and get a firm "yes" on each.

1. Is it desirable?

Does your target client want it? *Will it help get them from where they are now to where they want to be?* For example, you could say, "We specialize in wildly expensive interior design that always goes way over budget but guarantees you the most interesting stuff!" Great?! Except that won't fly with most potential clients. Every possible messaging point should be run through the "Is it desirable?" filter.

The client for one interior design business would love to go shopping with you and grab lunch. The client for another would rather have you stop by with an efficient presentation and then move on with their day. To figure out if a messaging point is desirable, you have to understand your target client.

If you've researched marketing for more than five minutes, you've heard all about the importance of having a specific target client, but maybe you're still not quite clear on yours.

One quick way to get that work started is to think about all of your past clients and choose one or two as avatars. An ideal target client works well with your systems, has the budget and timeline that you need to do your best work, appreciates your aesthetic or your ability to project their aesthetic, and, at the end of the day, yields a profit for your business.

Maybe you don't have an example of your typical client. It's possible that your business is young or you've been saying yes to certain demands when you should have been saying no, and you don't know your ideal avatar yet. You can still put together the characteristics of an ideal client on paper. Needless to say, they can't be a unicorn. They must exist in numbers large enough to support your business (this doesn't have to be a huge number—whatever works for your business model) and be able to access your services.

Once you have a target client in mind, you'll have the ability to think about possible messaging points and ask yourself, "Is this desirable to _____?"

2. Is it different?

Messaging doesn't state the obvious. If every designer in your city (or, more accurately, on planet Earth) is talking about "transforming spaces," it becomes absolutely meaningless. Why? Because that's what all interior designers do. It's boring to even talk about it right now.

When asking "Is it different?" it helps to know what your competitors are doing and saying. Sure, it's healthy to focus on your own business, but an awareness of the other players in your market is a must. Make a list: who else would potential clients look at when searching for an interior designer? Which designers are on your own radar? If you Google "interior designer (your city or area)," which businesses do you see? Go check out their websites and social media. What are they communicating?

Once you have a sense of what's out there, you'll start to form ideas on what sets you apart so that you can help the target client in their search. Think about it from their perspective: They don't want to research this for six months. In most cases, they just want to hire a good designer and get the job done.

How can we help this poor soul? By showing them points of differentiation.

What makes you different from your competitors can come in many categories, from price of services to years of experience. Here are a few types of points of differentiation to get you thinking:

- specific target client
- emphasis on a particular benefit of your services
- special credentials
- innovative design solutions
- innovative or unique process
- unique pricing structure
- agile project timelines
- specialization in specific building types or rooms
- special expertise in sourcing, assembling a crack team of craftspeople, etc.
- your own process or style of project management
- stellar service or offering some unique client support
- expertise in a particular style
- delightful little (or big) surprises
- a close personal relationship with Oprah, who will come to the reveal and give your client a hug (this would be pretty great)

A point of differentiation gives a client or prospect something to hold on to mentally—a way to bond with you before you even meet. For the right target client, messaging that says "Hey, this interior design firm does a thing that I value" is exactly what they've been searching for.

3. Is it doable?

You could put together some really desirable messaging right now ("We're the only interior design firm that will renovate your kitchen in two days just like they do on HGTV!"), but it has to be within the bounds of reality. Not only that, but every messaging point also has to feel good to you as the owner of the business. You need to be excited about it. And you have to be ready to prove it, which we'll discuss in a moment.

This is why the answer to all three questions must be a resounding yes. Even if it's desirable and different from your competitors, you may not want "super responsive" to be a messaging point. Why? Because you may not want to be locked into providing lightning-fast communication. Every business should be reasonably responsive, but if you're going to include something in your messaging, get ready to commit to it.

In working through this process, you are looking for elements of your brand that are (or can be) baked in, 100 percent true, and completely doable. You'll need everyone to be on board, from you to your employees to your contractors.

The process: Finding messaging points and refining

Now you know the criteria that tells you if a messaging point is right for you—but how do you actually get to the messaging points themselves? The short answer is this: You figure out your messaging by asking strategic questions and panning for gold within the answers.

Step 1: Answer the right questions

Start by sitting down with a notebook—digital or paper—and answering the following questions. A friendly warning: this will take time. Sit in your most comfortable chair, pour yourself a glass of wine, play your favorite focus music, and get ready for an awkward first date with your brand. Some of these questions will be easy. Some will require more thought or inspire new ideas. This will be work, but it is important work with huge returns.

- What areas do you serve?
- What services do you offer?
- What basic problems do you solve for your clients?
- How is your client's life better once they've worked with you?
- Think about one or two competitors. What do you do better/faster/smarter than them?
- Does your best work have certain elements in common? What are they?
- Are there certain words that your clients consistently use to describe you? (Check testimonials, if available.)
- What service would you like to sell more of?
- Why do clients hire you instead of another designer?
- How do you surprise your clients?
- Do you see any opportunities in the marketplace? Anything you could take advantage of?
- You are the ONLY designer in this area who …
- Your process is special in this way …
- What does your target client need to know about you in order to trust you?
- If you could dream big, what would your business look like?

(Visit curioelectro.com/messaging for a printable version of these questions and a checklist for the entire messaging process.)

Step 2: Ask your target client to answer the right questions

Now go back to your ideal target client. You're looking for someone who you wish would send you a dozen friends just like them. Select two of your best clients and ask them (politely and with much gratitude for taking the time) to provide answers to these questions:

- How did you find me?
- What was your main goal in hiring an interior designer?

- When did you know that you had made the right decision by hiring me?
- Would you recommend me? Why and to whom?
- If you spoke with (or worked with) other designers, what made you choose me for your project?
- What do you feel is special about my services?
- What three words would you use to describe me?

Step 3: Pressure test the things you learn against three criteria

This is where it starts to get interesting. Begin by assembling all of your findings in one place. Grab a pen and get to work:

- **Is it desirable?** Sweep through all of the answers looking for interesting tidbits that are desirable to your target client. Underline them.
- **Is it different?** Sweep through the answers again, this time looking for mentions of things that make you different than your competitors or the interior design industry at large. Underline them.
- **Is it doable?** Scan your answers one more time. There should be items that have already filled the requirements for desirable and different. Are they also doable? Underline them.

Anything that has been underlined three times is a potential messaging point.

Step 4: Refine

Once you have some potential messaging points, you'll want to copy them onto a new document and refine them. Simplify the wording and double-check to make sure that nothing is vague or meaningless.

Some examples are shown below. A few of the "good" messaging points may seem slightly crazy to you, and that's exactly how it should be. These are not your messaging points. They're imaginary. But they're specific and could fulfill the requirements of desirable, different, and doable for the right interior designer and target client:

Examples of Good Messaging Points	Examples of Bad Messaging Points
• Relationships with every great contractor and craftsperson in Portland • Unusually intuitive with clients during the design process • Expertise in library design or eco-friendly kitchens • Flat fee pricing, including furnishings • Known for innovative, gorgeous storage solutions • Specializing in high-end contemporary design • Clients get a lesson on styling at the end of the project • Proven track record of staying on budget and on time	• Freshens the look of a home • Transforms a space • Nice to work with (You get the idea!)

Messaging is all talk until you prove it.

Now comes the most important step in this process: once you have your messaging defined, you must make it real. Actually, don't just make it real—blow it up. Make it fifty percent more true than when you decided it should be a messaging point in the first place.

PROVE your messaging by making it three-dimensional. You can do that in a number of places:

Web and Print Copy: This may be the lowest-hanging fruit, but it matters. When someone visits your website, do they understand what makes you different and why they should hire you? If one of your messaging points is that you specialize in working with busy, two-income couples with big careers, are they reading words that speak directly to their needs?

This does not have to be—and, much of the time, *should not* be—literal. ("Interior design for busy, two-income couples with big careers!") It's about addressing their pain points: Tell them that you are the only designer in the area with a process that is crafted for clients with complex schedules. Acknowledge the importance of a home that functions well when you return from traveling or a long day. Feature testimonials from this type of client. Speak their language.

The person who writes your website copy—whether it is you or a professional copywriter—should start with and come back to your messaging points. Not every piece of messaging should be stated in writing (keep reading for other ways to prove messaging points), but your messaging will serve as the foundation for your tagline, the words on your home page, ad copy, and more.

Storytelling: If you say that you deliver best-in-class service to your clients, that's great. It's possible that someone might believe you, right? But if you tell *a story* that paints a picture of delivering amazing service, not only will they believe you, but they will also remember the story. A messaging point that is illustrated through story becomes true in the minds of those who hear it. It acts as proof.

Once you have defined your messaging points, sit down with them and look for the stories. Keep them on hand and look for the right places to tell them.

Blog Posts: When you see the word "blog," do you think "hard work with no discernable return on investment"? That's understandable, if you don't have clear messaging in place. The good news is that once you define your messaging, a blog becomes an excellent delivery vehicle to put you and your brand out into the world.

If you specialize in a particular aesthetic, it should be all over your blog. If you have expertise in kitchen design, tell your readers how to prepare for a kitchen renovation. If your process is unique, write a post about it (with images and stories) and send that link to prospective clients. If you are a Boston designer and that's part of your messaging, showcase other local businesses who work in parallel industries such as architecture or wine. As you search out topics for your posts, always look to your messaging for inspiration.

Photo Selection: It may be a cliché, but it's still the best approach: Choose quality over quantity. Remember, you are telling a story with your portfolio page, the images you choose for your home page, and even the images you post on social media. What's the story? Let your messaging guide you.

If you specialize in a particular niche or aesthetic, boldly proclaim that with your photo editing. Your portfolio is, after all, not so much a record of your previous projects as it is a predictor of your future ones.

If you want to communicate that you specialize in whole-house projects, then don't group your projects by room (kitchens, bathrooms, etc.). Group them by project. Tell a visual story and, whenever possible, prove your messaging.

Systems: This is one of the most powerful aspects of this process, so get ready to create some magic. Injecting messaging into your systems makes it real to your clients. When clients experience the aspects of your brand that you want to communicate, they spread your messaging for you. "Innovative storage solutions in every project" becomes an actual, real benefit when your processes are solidly built to include and highlight it every time. Make sure your client realizes when the magic is happening.

If you say that you constantly surprise your clients, build that into your systems with a gift halfway through the project and/or by sourcing of a custom piece of art. If you say that you deliver stunningly good service, build that into your systems with great onboarding and a help desk with quick response time. Think big. Get creative. Then get nerdy and specific about implementation.

Employee Training: Once an employee or contractor understands what you're known for, they'll have the tools to make some of the smaller decisions on their own.

Create a training for employees so that they understand all of your messaging points. Make sure they're on board with your systems. Put together a three-sentence, "this is our thing" speech for your vendors and contractors. Anyone who represents your business in the world will benefit from understanding your messaging.

Testimonials: Testimonials are powerful because, in the very beginning of the relationship, other people's words are more trustworthy than yours. Asking for a testimonial should be included in your project task list. Highlight the ones that speak to your messaging points. Or take it one step further by using a feedback form and asking questions that prompt them to discuss topics that relate your messaging or will likely yield something specific and interesting:

- What is your favorite piece in the room? Why?
- What was your favorite part of working with us?
- Optional: If you felt that we delivered excellent service, can you provide an example?

Social Media Posts: Ah, social media. Whether you're creating free posts or using paid ads, social media is an excellent way to get in front of people who don't know you yet and nurture relationships with those who do.

If you want to be memorable, make sure you are injecting messaging into every post. Everything mentioned above applies: edit your images with messaging in mind, caption your images with stories and references to messaging points, and theme your posts around messaging points. Stop blending in and start taking up a spot in the minds of your audience.

But, what if ...?

> A: *"I service a target client who values privacy and prefers an interior design firm that is not all over social media. 'Putting my messaging out into the world' goes against that, right?"*

If part of your messaging is that you value the privacy of your clients, then that point should be proven just like any other. Mention it in your website copy, note that you were given permission by a client when posting an image on social media, and be very selective about where you advertise. As always, know what is desirable to your target client and then prove that you are truly doing it.

> B: *"I serve a small market and I'm afraid to come off too niche or alienate any potential clients."*

Every business needs messaging, but the nature of that messaging will depend on what is desirable to your market. If you are in a smaller market—let's say a more rural area where there simply are not enough potential clients to support specializing in a niched down, specific aesthetic—then a declaration that you only work with clients who want industrial interior design in their foyers might not fit the "desirable" requirement.

Your messaging must tick off all three boxes: desirable, different, and doable. In smaller markets, the messaging may focus more on level of service, process, unique design packages, ability to source or customize, and so on.

C: *"I just started this business and I have no idea what is special about my services."*

Honestly, it can take a little time to figure this stuff out. In order to ask clients what is special about you, it helps to have some clients. To understand who your target client is, it helps to have a few projects under your belt. That being said, there are interior designers who start their business with a clear vision or have it all nailed down after a year. No matter who you are—starting a business today or thirty years in—clearly identifying your messaging points will be a game-changer. And, just like anything, else, messaging can be tweaked over time.

D: *"I've looked at a ton of interior designers' websites and many of them don't seem to have much messaging or, often, many words on the home page. Why should I be different?"*

Because interior design is a business just like any other. If you want to move beyond referrals and ensure you are taking full advantage of every referral that comes your way, it is to your benefit to give potential clients a specific, understandable reason to call you. The fact that you're seeing interior design businesses without messaging or a cohesive brand is GREAT because it means you will be leaps and bounds beyond them in your marketing efforts.

Simply put: messaging matters.

Not to be grandiose, but what makes you different is what can turn you into an interior design icon. Find your messaging. Let everyone know about it. That's how you define your brand.

I forgot to tell you up front that Nicole is also hilariously funny, she cracks me up constantly, but you probably figured that out by now for yourself.

Grab your wine and have your first date with your brand. If you do the exercises Nicole gave us, you will make headway on understanding your message. However, what's that saying? Don't mistake simple for easy. This applies here. Nicole breaks it down for us in simple, direct steps, but you have some work to do. If your criteria for mastering your brand message is that it should be quick and easy to do, you're probably not going to be successful.

I have said it on the show: Nicole's process for understanding your messaging is like going through therapy for your business. If you think of it in these terms, then you can see that it is something that you have to take time to do. As with therapy, when you are honest with yourself, when you elicit the help and opinions of those close to you—in this case your clients— and you put in the work, coming out the other side is incredibly rewarding. It leads to self-awareness, growth, and confidence, which are all well worth the time and effort.

In my first book, I told the story about the woman who found us through a Facebook group. Because it is such a perfect example of when you have your brand so clearly defined that when your clients talk about you, they say the exact things you say about your company, I'll share an abbreviated version here too.

I was meeting with a potential client and in conversation I asked her how she heard about Window Works. She explained that she asked in her local newcomer's Facebook group if anyone would recommend someone for custom window treatments. She said in the first twenty minutes, nearly two dozen people said to call Window Works. Well naturally this made me very happy, and I smiled proudly. Then she quite deliberately looked at me and said, "Well, not every comment was so good." Hmm, ok, I asked her what the not-so-good comments were. She described that the few negative comments all said the same thing, that we were expensive.

Taking this in, I said to her, "Would you tell me what the people who recommended us said about Window Works?"

Answering me she said, "Oh yes! Everything from, you do such excellent work, you are family owned, you have been in the community for years, your service is outstanding, and you design beautiful window treatments. One woman even described how your installer had two pairs of shoes with him on her rainy-day installation. One that he put on as he went outside to his truck each trip, and the other he put on as he worked inside her home!"

I looked at her, directly in the eye, and said, "Do you want to trade all of that for a lower price?"

This is an undeniable direct example of Nicole's prompt sentence in her chapter:

"Window Works is the company that is family owned and operated for nearly four decades and delivers excellent quality products and exceptional customer service."

Our tag line at Window Works is "Experience, Expertise, Excellence."

This is what we say about ourselves, and, most importantly, it is what our clients say about us. It is pretty powerful when you hear your clients tell you what you are known for, and it is precisely what you strive to be every day, through each team member, with every client.

Now it is time for you, with Nicole's help and guidance, to figure out what you say about your interior design firm and for you to show and deliver to your clients so they will say it about you, too.

- LN

About the Author

Nicole Heymer is the founder of Curio Electro, a boutique creative agency specializing in intuitive branding, compelling design, and actionable plans. Since 2011, Curio Electro has worked with a wide variety of clients at every stage in their development, from nationally known interior design firms to local craft breweries. Nicole's clear, practical take on branding has been featured in print, on podcasts, and as the framework for branding workshops.

Nicole has appeared on LuAnn's podcast twice, on episodes 125 and 317:

https://luannnigara.com/125-nicole-heymer-brand-business/

https://luannnigara.com/317-nicole-heymer-6-keys-to-planning-a-website-that-makes-things-happen/

CHAPTER 2

Peter Lang

I just love that Peter Lang is, quite literally, *The Designer's CPA. The way you, as a designer, do business is a different model than the average product- or service-based business. The myriad of income streams, from consultations to design fees to product sales, are complicated and are difficult to navigate. Knowing that Peter only accepts interior design clients ensures that he fully understands the complexity of our industry. This is why I invited Peter to write a chapter in my book. I have interviewed several CPAs and have admired and valued each one, but—let's be serious—the business side of interior design is not for the meek of heart. Knowing that Peter genuinely loves working with the interior designer's business model put him right at the top of my list.*

In this chapter, Peter gives us specific criteria for selecting a CPA as well as helpful questions to ask once you are ready to interview a few. His insights are right on the mark.

- LN

Find the Best Accountant for Your Design Firm

By Peter Lang

A Tale of Two Designers

On a gorgeous morning in May, ten years ago, two designers graduated from the New York School of Interior Design. Although they traveled in different circles, they were similar in many ways. They were dedicated to their craft, confident in the future, eager to build their portfolios and eager to eventually start their own design firms.

Almost like clockwork, five years after graduating and working tirelessly in the field under major design firms, the designers each launched their own business.

A decade after graduating, the designers attended their college reunion. Although ten years had passed, they were still alike in many ways. They had both continued to work in the design field and help their clients create beautiful spaces that suited their unique personalities.

There was one major difference.

One of the designers was asked to speak at the reunion about how she created a six-figure business in just five years after going out on her own and was on track to hit seven figures next year. The other designer had closed the doors on his dream after three arduous years in business and was back working for a design firm.

What Made the Difference?

Have you ever wondered what the difference is between a successful business owner and one who started a business, only to shut it down a few years after opening?

Ask anyone why some businesses fail and others succeed and you'll get as many different answers as people you ask. Often, people assume that in order to be successful, designers must:

- Have a boatload of cash to launch their business
- Niche down to a very specific segment of the market
- Spend a fortune on marketing
- Have connections with wealthy clients
- Have a team of employees working to support their business and clients
- Become an authority by publishing a book on design or speaking at the hottest trade shows
- Work eighty-hour weeks while neglecting their family and relationships
- Be the Greatest of All Time when it comes to organization, leadership, and time management

Are some of these factors helpful in sustaining a successful design business? Absolutely. However, many of them are just excuses or rationalizations that business owners tell themselves to help ease the pain and utter defeat that can accompany the close of a business.

As a CPA working solely with clients in the design industry, I see successful business owners and I see designers who are in a constant state of anxiety, wondering if this the year they'll have to close the doors forever.

As an entrepreneur myself, it's excruciating to see business owners embark on their journey with the best intentions, only to crumble under financial pressure. On my worst days, I've had to deliver news to clients, such as:

- They will not profit because they've overspent or mismanaged their budget.
- The money they invested in their business did not yield any ROI and actually worked against them.
- They owe the government money because they didn't set their business up properly for tax purposes.
- A simple sales tax error has substantially diminished their profit.

Fortunately, I don't have to deliver bad news often. The majority of my clients own profitable businesses. I work with them as a part-time CFO, developing a strategy to scale their business, deliver more value to customers, and, as a result, command a higher rate.

This is no accident.

I'd like to tell you that it's because the anxiety-inducing statistic that fifty percent of new businesses fail within their first five years is false. That I have a rigorous client intake process that prevents me from taking on struggling business owners, so I never, *ever*, have to deliver bad news. I'd be thrilled to tell you that I work mostly with successful designers because I'm the best CPA on the planet. That when designers walk into my office it's all … POW! BOOM! BANG! and the profits just pour into their bank account.

Unfortunately, none of that is true.

While some of my clients have told me I'm the world's greatest CPA for *them* (we'll get to this later), the reason goes back to the story at the beginning of this chapter: **There is one major difference between successful business owners and those on the cusp of a financial crisis.**

It explains exactly how two designers who graduated from the exact same college, with access to the same opportunities and financial means, had wildly different business outcomes.

It's the secret that you never learned in school, one that rails against the traditional and accepted practice. The answer to the age-old question of why some business owners make it, while others crash and burn is simple: **Successful business owners know that in order to profit, they *must* make time to meet with their CPA on a *consistent and regular* basis. They know that the conventional belief of only needing to meet with your CPA at tax time is a complete and utter sham.**

We all know people who only visit their accountant when it's tax time. If you're being honest, you might even be someone who does this.

Let me be clear. If you're a business owner who is completely committed to building a profitable, financially stable design business, you must flat-out reject the idea of meeting with your accountant once per year. **This idea will bankrupt you.**

I say this not to be a fearmonger. I've seen passionate business owners, who care deeply about serving clients and growing their business, fail because they don't know the numbers. They only call their CPA once a year, during tax time. Don't let the common misconception that CPAs only want to work with clients during tax time sink your business.

Of course, it's not only designers who avoid the accountant. In fact, it's more common to hear about people avoiding the accountant than looking forward to meeting with their accountant. It should be the opposite. A good accountant (I'll tell you exactly what to look for in yours) acts as a profitability partner.

The misconception that accountants are money-hungry mutants sent by the IRS, with the sole duty of sucking up your hard-earned salary, is still out there.

The myth that you should meet with your accountant annually, during tax time is so widespread and ingrained in us. **In my experience, this belief stems from one, or both of the following reasons:**

- **Learned behavior:** This happens when your beliefs are ingrained in you from a young age. Maybe your parents never visited the accountant, only made an appointment to get their taxes done, or only visited when something was wrong. As a result, you started to believe that everyone should only see their accountant annually or when you're in financial trouble.

  Perhaps you experienced family members or friends who were completely stressed out after visiting the accountant only to discover that they were on the hook for hundreds or thousands of dollars. One, let alone several, experiences like this will reinforce the societal belief that visiting your accountant is an unpleasant and often financially draining experience.

- **Comfort:** For some of you, it might be easier **not** to know what's going on with your day-to-day financials. A theme I see over and over again with my design clients is the belief that they aren't good with numbers. They view their accountant as an outside entity rather than a profitability partner. This is a faulty foundation on which to build a relationship. You can't just outsource the entire accounting arm of your business to your CPA. There are basic reports that you need to familiarize yourself with in order to be successful.

This is not for your accountant's well-being or to make it easier for your accountant to work with you. It's crucial to the financial success of your business. As I said earlier, what you don't know will hurt you. When you work with a good accountant, they will show you how to get comfortable with what's uncomfortable or not natural for you, i.e., the numbers.

It's important to remember that if you fall into the category of business owners who only see their accountant once a year, it's not too late. Your business is not doomed. There's no reason to beat yourself up.

The fact that you're reading this book is proof positive that you're invested in the well-being of your business. Read it from cover to cover. Then, if you haven't read LuAnn's first book, *The Making of A Well-Designed Business*®, read that too. The wisdom you glean from these two books will help you understand how to run a successful design business.

That's not all though. Not even close. **For any of this to work, you must do something:**

You must ACT! Take what you learn in these pages and carry it out in your business. You've heard the expression that knowledge is power. That's only one side of the equation. The real power comes from taking what you learn and acting on it.

If you commit to acting on what you learn in these pages, the results will be transformative. You'll come to realize that not only is knowledge power, but also that acting on it will catapult your business into profitability.

Do You Need an Accountant?

I read LuAnn's first book prior to meeting her. The second chapter of the book focuses on what she calls "Your Dream Team." In her list of "nonnegotiable experts," she lists a tax coach and accountant. Her sage advice on pages 14-15 of *The Making of A Well-Designed Business®* is worth repeating:

> **Tax coach and accountant.** Think of an accountant like the doctor you see for your yearly checkup. This doctor will analyze your weight, your cholesterol level, your blood pressure, your heart rate, your sugar level, etc. Then he or she will tell you your test results and give you some advice on things you should cut back on or do more of until you see each other again in a year. He or she will monitor you yearly and simply document your results.
>
> Now think of a tax coach like a personal trainer. The personal trainer breaks down your yearly health goals into weekly and monthly action lists and teaches you the exercises you need to do and the foods you need to eat. This person works by your side, making sure you execute the proper steps and helping you achieve your goals, and provides the accountability that the MD does not. This way, at the end of the year, when you go for your checkup with the MD, you are healthy.
>
> So, the accountant will record, monitor, and prepare your financial documents quarterly and yearly, and the tax coach will strategize and guide you one-on-one throughout the year. Over the years, as you become more knowledgeable, you will need the tax coach less often; however, you will always need the accountant.
>
> Sometimes, your accountant might also be your tax coach, but if your accountant simply "records" what you have done each year,

please find yourself a tax coach in addition to your accountant. It's paramount to understand what to do throughout the year so you are prepared at year-end. And being prepared at year-end means you are not only financially legal but also financially solvent.

Some things to cover with the tax coach and an accountant include:

- Determining the best classification for your business. Examples include S-Corp, LLC, and sole proprietorship. There are advantages and disadvantages to each, and you need to understand them to make the proper choice for you.
- Learning how to set up a daily accounting system, whether it's something like FreshBooks or something of your own. The point is, you must have a daily financial system, and you must use it from day one. Don't wait until your first year in business comes to a close and then find out what you were supposed to have done all year long to be ready for the taxman.
- Determining how and when you personally should expect to take a paycheck from your business. It's not uncommon for small business owners to go weeks and months before taking a paycheck. Often this is because you are reinvesting the profits into the business, which can be a good thing as long as it's monitored and thoughtfully tracked with specific goals planned. But make no mistake: Running a business is not a hobby. And if you don't earn a living from it, it's a hobby—a very expensive hobby. I always say, if I want a hobby, I'll hit my yoga class! Be intentional about how you will make money from your business.

As you can see, the answer to the question of whether you need an accountant is a resounding "yes." You need an accountant and a tax coach, preferably both (who can be either the same person or two different people) if you want a well-designed business. These roles are on your nonnegotiable list. In order to run your business smoothly, you need to fill these roles.

If you're still wondering why on earth you need the right accountant, one who's focused on your business, experienced in your industry, and actually cares about what's going on, consider Jessica.

Jessica reached out to me after stumbling on my website. She had never worked with an accountant experienced in the design industry and wanted to know more. Before our call, I briefly researched Jessica's company online. On her website she had multiple interior design awards listed and a ton of testimonials from satisfied clients.

As an accountant, I have trouble even referring to looking at Jessica's website as "research." I had zero access to her numbers or financial data, so my conclusion was not at all scientific. Still, for all intents and purposes, I thought Jessica's business was doing well, at least in the school of public opinion.

Imagine my surprise when she started off our meeting on the verge of tears.

Jessica's accountant had just informed her that she owed more than twenty thousand dollars in taxes. Even a cold-hearted sadist shouldn't deliver such horrific news without lessening the blow with ways to avoid such a massive charge in the future.

All it took was a few questions before I was able to tell Jessica why this happened and how she could save a tremendous amount of money in the future.

Fact: The way you form your business has the potential to deplete your profits or save you thousands of dollars each year.

Jessica ended up firing her sadist accountant. Our first order of business together was to change her business structure. This simple switch ended up shaving fifteen thousand dollars off her tax payment annually! Imagine saving fifteen thousand dollars *and* getting an accountant who understands your business and monitors it. It's a no-brainer!

A good accountant will help you decide how to structure your business. It doesn't matter if you're not currently structured correctly; you can restructure at any time.

Here are the different ways most of my clients structure their businesses.

LLC: A common and ideal way to structure your business and keep it separate from your personal assets. An LLC, or Limited Liability Corporation, protects you in the unlikely, though not impossible, event that a client sues you. This structure ensures your home and all your personal assets are protected.

Sole Proprietor: Clients tend to pick this structure based on the name alone, thinking that they must be a sole proprietor if they're self-employed. The problem with this structure is that there's no separation between your personal assets and your business liabilities. Therefore, if a disgruntled client thinks you've completely botched the job and wants to sue you for everything you own, they can. And by everything, I mean *everything*. This includes your house, everything in it, your car … the list goes on.

Partnership: A partnership is very similar to a sole proprietor, but instead of one person, there are multiple people, or "partners," responsible for all aspects of the business.

S Corp (or Corporation): Designers who file as an S Corp or a corporation are subject to more formalities than an LLC. An S Corp typically has shareholders, owners, and directors and is required to meet at least annually.

Now that you see why you absolutely need an accountant and tax coach, let's talk about finding the best accountant for you.

How to Find the Best Accountant for Your Business

As I said earlier, my clients have told me before that I'm the best accountant. While I'd like to pat myself on the back for that, I know the truth. I am the best accountant *for them*.

The designers who are happy about our working arrangement didn't simply Google "tax accountants," select the first accountant in the list, and call it a day. They were much more intentional about their choice. They met with me prior to signing on as a client. They asked me questions to see if I was the right fit for their business. They made sure they were selecting an accountant who was familiar with the design industry and who was able to help them achieve their goals.

Here's a simple three-step process to help you choose the right CPA.

1. **Ask friends in the design industry for referrals to a CPA they trust,** specifically one with experience with design and cloud-based accounting software.

2. **Interview the CPA prior to working together.** Ask questions such as:

   a. *What designers do you currently work with?* **Tip:** You want an accountant experienced in your industry. Ask open-ended questions that elicit more than a yes or no answer. This will give you more insight into their experience and comfort working in the design industry.

   b. *Can you tell me about your experience working in design software?* You want to ask about the software you use specifically.

   c. *How is your relationship with different bookkeepers?* **Remember:** your accountant is your profitability partner, one that will help you get to the next level in your business. Most CPAs, including myself, focus on the bigger financial picture and helping you achieve the goals you set for your business. While we don't input all your income and expenses, we absolutely need this information to help you meet your goals. A good working relationship between your accountant and your bookkeeper is crucial.

   d. *Can you give me an example of when you needed to help a designer navigate differences in sales tax?*

   e. *How often do you typically meet with your clients?* **Tip:** If they say once, or only during tax time, run. At the very least, you want to meet with your accountant on a quarterly basis.

   f. *How do you charge?* You want to make sure you're not getting slammed with charges for every phone call to your accountant.

3. **Use the interview to gauge not only the accountant's experience, but their interpersonal style.** Do you feel comfortable asking questions, or does their response or tone make you feel insignificant or dumb? **Tip:** A successful relationship with your accountant requires open communication on both parts. It's a two-way street, requiring both of you to feel comfortable being honest with each other. Ask yourself, "Could I work with this person? Would I feel comfortable asking them questions?"

Now it's go time!

Use the process outlined above and find a great accountant for your business. Make sure you're looking not only for the "right" answers, but also for a good fit for you. You need to feel comfortable asking questions, even questions that you might feel silly asking. Remember, what you don't know about your financials *will* hurt you.

Once you've found the perfect accountant for your business, it's time to talk about your first meeting.

Your First Date with an Accountant

By now you know that your relationship with your accountant needs to be one where there's open communication. Consider it a real relationship. Your first meeting (after deciding they were the best accountant for you) is similar to a first date. How do you act, what do you say or do? What do you make sure to include or avoid in order to make a good impression?

Four ways to ensure the first date with your accountant is great.

1. **Prepare.** You already know how important image is. Harness your signature style and attention to detail to prepare for your first meeting. Bring anything that you think would be helpful for your new accountant to understand your business. This might include:
   a. Your past year of business savings and checking statements
   b. Project and accounting software credentials so you can login and show your accountant what you've been tracking
   c. Your bookkeeper's name and contact information
   d. Your biggest challenges and/or goals for your business in the next fiscal year
   e. And more, depending on what your accountant expects you to bring. Tip: the only way to find out is to ask them, *before* your meeting!
2. **Listen.** Similar to a first date, you want to make sure you're actually listening to your accountant versus zoning out, looking at your phone, or being otherwise distracted. You'll be expecting the same respect and consideration from them, so be sure to reciprocate.
3. **Participate.** Like any solid relationship, it takes two people to make it work. The same goes for your relationship with your accountant. Give your accountant what they need to help you. Take their knowledge and help and use it to grow and scale.
4. **Ask questions!** One of the most common mistakes threatening the accountant/client relationship is the client's inability to ask questions, for fear of sounding stupid. Imagine you're back in high school with that teacher who reminded you ad infinitum, *there's no such thing as a stupid question* while peering over her glasses. It's true. Yes, even for those of you who exasperatedly exclaim, "I just don't do numbers." If you don't ask questions, you won't be able to give your accountant what they need to do their job. If your accountant can't do their job, then not only are you wasting your hard-earned money, you're missing out on massive profits for your business.

How NOT to Sabotage Your Relationship with Your Accountant and Deplete Your Profits

We didn't come this far only to come this far, right? Unfortunately, even after selecting a great accountant and having a productive kick-off meeting, some designers still manage to swerve off track—straight into a profitability pothole.

You, dear reader, will *not* do this. Repeat after me: *The relationship with my accountant is a two-way street. In order to profit, I must give my accountant what they need to do their job. I must listen to them, ask for clarification if I don't understand, and follow the recommendations we come up with collectively.*

Rule 1: The best relationships are partnerships, where both parties actively work to move the relationship forward. You already know that asking questions when you need clarification is a *must*. Often, when you and your accountant make decisions, you'll be required to help make that decision a reality. Whether it's getting your CPA what they need or signing documents, just do it. Complete your responsibilities in a timely manner, without having to be asked hundreds of times. In doing so, you'll prove to your accountant that you're invested in your business. In turn, your CPA will be more invested and you'll get better results. *Cha-ching!*

Rule 2: Do not mistake your CPA for Harry Houdini. As I stated above, your accountant needs information from you to accurately assess your financial situation and help manage it. Did you receive a letter in the mail from the IRS? Review it, then immediately forward it via email to your CPA with any information you think would be helpful. Just snap a picture of it on your phone, send via email and include relevant notes. Keep the lines of communication open at all times.

Rule 3: You still have to deal with numbers. This is, by far, the most common mistake I see designers make in their business. They let their aversion to numbers stop them from working with their accountant.

42

Want the cold, hard truth? **Numbers are the lifeblood of your business.**

There's an old adage you may have heard: *If you don't know your numbers, you don't know your business.* For some reason, creatives don't like to hear this. If I had a dollar for every time I've heard something along the lines of: *I hired you so I don't have to deal with numbers!* I'd have enough money to fund an all-expenses paid trip to Disney for my wife and our twin boys.

The fact is, knowing your numbers and understanding some very basic reports *will* give you the tools to make smarter, more economical decisions. When my clients listen and start to understand their financials, the magic happens. Most of the time they start making better decisions almost unconsciously. Just knowing their numbers affects how they spend their money on a daily basis.

I'm not talking calculus here, folks.

All you need is an understanding of a few basic reports, including:

- **Balance sheet:** This report shows you all of your assets and liabilities, so you have an overall picture of what's happening in your business.
- **Income statement:** Your income statement will detail your monthly, quarterly, and yearly profit and loss statements.
- **Accounts receivable:** Never miss a payment again! When you understand the accounts receivable report, you understand what clients are outstanding and how long they've been outstanding for.
- **Accounts payable:** You like to get paid and so do your vendors. The accounts payable report shows all your outstanding bills, along with the due dates. Pay your vendors on time to show them you value their service and the relationship. Oh, and to ensure they don't cut you off!
- **Cash flow:** This report is key in understanding how cash is moving throughout your business. Moreover, it helps you monitor any increase or decrease in cash flow.

- **Sales tax:** You know the importance of sales tax and understanding how it fluctuates depending on jurisdiction. The sales tax report will help you decipher how much sales tax is owed on a certain project.

Rule 4: Consult your CPA *before* you spend large sums of money. Congratulations! Your client handed you a fat check and your bank account looks better than it has, well, *ever!*

Now, repeat after me: *This cash is not all mine. I need to allocate it. This cash is not all mine. I need to allocate it.*

Want to fast-track your business to financial trouble? Here's how:

Your client hands you a sizeable deposit upfront for a job. You're thrilled and breathe a sigh of relief because:

- Your bills are due or even overdue;
- You're finally getting the clients you want and deserve! There's no better way to portray your newfound success then rolling up to your next client meeting in a fancy new car;
- You need to cover costs on a job that you didn't properly allocate funds for, i.e. borrowing Peter to pay Paul; or
- You rationalize that it's just a small loan and you'll be able to reimburse the account before it's time to purchase materials for the client's job.

If this hasn't happened to you, give yourself a pat on the back for being part of the minority.

If you find yourself gazing proudly at a large sum of money in your bank account and dreaming about the possibilities, it's time to call your accountant. Your accountant will help you make an informed decision about whether you truly need whatever it is you're hankering for. You'll arrive at your answer with actual financial information and data to either support it or not.

Logical, rational decisions aren't always fun. Still, it's your accountant's duty to help you make the best fiscal decisions for your business. Just imagine how much fun you'll have when you're at the helm of a profitable, thriving design business!

Rule 5: Invest in your partnership and demand the same from your accountant. The final way to ensure that your relationship with your accountant is a prosperous one is to continually monitor it. By now, you've learned that the foundation of a successful accountant/designer relationship is a mutual partnership, where both of you work towards the same goal. It's a delicate balance of give and take that requires both parties to take action and shoulder responsibility.

If you find yourself feeling as though you're giving more than you're receiving from your accountant, take a step back from the situation. Try to honestly and objectively assess the situation. Have you been providing your accountant with the information that they need to be effective? If it's a situation that negatively impacted your financials, was there anything you could have done to prevent it? If you're having trouble being objective, consider enlisting the opinion of a trusted friend.

A one-sided relationship is never productive or profitable. If, after laying out all the facts, you conclude that your accountant is not acting in your best interest, it's time to cut them loose and find another.

Your accountant is a key player in helping you achieve profitability and success. They are a nonnegotiable member of your dream team. When you find the right one, you'll see how quickly this relationship will transform your business.

Of all of the advice Peter shared, the three things that stand out to me the most are:

- *You must be an informed, involved partner in your finances.*
- *You must meet with your CPA more than once per year.*
- *You must be able to ask any question at all and not be made to feel dumb about it.*

Think about it. When you work with a client, often you see right away they have little or no sense for color, scale or style. Would you ever speak to them in a superior or dismissive tone? Would you disregard their insecurities about interior design and treat them intimidatingly? No, you would not. You understand this is exactly why they need you: you understand these things so that they don't have to. Additionally, in designing their space, you explain how and why this sofa instead of that sofa, this tile over that tile. It is not a bother to you to help them understand the principles you use to design quality spaces. It is what you love to do—you love to help your clients achieve their design goals.

Don't settle for any less respect and effort when you seek out a CPA, a lawyer, or any other professional you need to run your firm. I sometimes find that because the balance sheet, the tax forms, and all of the finance things are "so official" that we think someone who understands this must be superior to us. No way! It is not true. They just have a different super power than us. They got the numbers gene and we got the spatial gene.

If you feel at a disadvantage in talking about your finances, or it seems intimidating to find and evaluate a CPA, please arrange to interview at least three. I want you to set up the interview for all three before you meet the first one. By interviewing more than one, you give yourself the best chance to find the CPA who is right for you.

You can and you will find that kind, smart, helpful CPAs just like Peter do exist. CPAs who want to partner with you and help you grow your business. It may take a few to find that one, and that's the reason I want you to have all three appointments set before interviewing. It will be much easier not to commit to hiring someone when you can truthfully say, "I have two other interviews, but I'll let you know what I decide."

Geography isn't an issue anymore either. With Skype, Zoom, and FaceTime, you can work remotely with your CPA. If you have a designer colleague miles and miles from you who loves her CPA, ask for the name. Of course, Peter works remotely as well. There is no excuse for not having someone who is qualified, respectful, encouraging, and as interested in your success as you are. If you have avoided hiring a CPA or you have neglected to establish ground rules with your CPA for any reason, please decide to make this a priority now. Whether you need a "let's reframe this relationship" conversation with your current CPA or you need to find a new CPA, please do it. This is a nonnegotiable expert on your business team.

- LN

About the Author

Peter Lang, CPA, is the founder of The Designer CPA, a firm that works exclusively with business owners in the design industry. He has worked in public accounting since 2002. Peter currently resides in Rhode Island with his wife and their identical twin boys. He enjoys running and golfing outside of work.

Peter appeared on LuAnn's podcast, episode 349:

https://luannnigara.com/349-power-talk-friday-peter-lang-the-designer-cpa/

CHAPTER 3

Michele Williams

Michele's superpower and passion is helping creatives like us rewrite the words of that bad song running through our mind: "I'm not good at the business side because I'm a creative person."

It truly breaks my heart, and I know from many conversations with Michele it breaks hers as well, to watch designers go on year after year and never run the business side effectively and never actually make a profit.

It truly is possible to stay open for years and never actually make money. Sadly, many do just that. Month after month, year after year, designers take deposits on product that they use to pay the gas and electric, only for the next month to arrive when they have to scrape together the money for the product invoices. Exhausted, frustrated entrepreneurs repeat this excruciating, stressful cycle for decades. They stay half of a step ahead of the bill collector, but two steps behind a healthy balance sheet.

Please do not be the business owner that pretends to themselves that because they are open and because somehow things get paid eventually, they are a business. This is just moving money in and out, robbing Peter to pay Paul. In this self-defeating, maddening cycle, you cannot forecast your income, which means you cannot plan for savings, for marketing, for business development, for new hires, or for a vacation.

In Michele's chapter, you will learn that, while she may have been somewhat more prepared by her previous experiences than most of us to run a business, she too struggled when it came to being profitable.

Knowing Michele also came to these financial lessons the hard way might be as powerful as the principles she teaches us. I think it gives hope that it is possible, that you do not, and you should not, accept financial failure because you are a creative.

Pay attention to how each year, she faced a new setback. She had some big-time "looking in the mirror" moments, which may surprise you knowing Michele now and knowing how expert she is in teaching us how to run our business for profit. One compelling difference exists between Michele and those who struggle year after year that cannot be overlooked or underestimated. Michele never once accepted the failures or the disappointments as something to be expected "because she didn't understand the numbers." Instead, with each setback, she dug in further, seeking, learning, and challenging herself to be and do better.

Michele was determined to make a profit.

Both Michele and I want that for you too.

- LN

Planning for Profit at Every Step
By Michele Williams

Profit is not an accident.

This statement takes some digesting because it means that becoming profitable might take just a bit more time than expected. It means wrapping your mind around the concept that you want to go beyond the *idea* of being profitable in your business and make a commitment to the *act* of doing what it takes to be profitable. In other words, it's one thing to *want* profitability, but it's another to be *committed* to the journey towards profitability; you must follow through the whole process to attain profitability. This is the crux of the outcome: if you want to be profitable, then you must stay the course—even when it all seems to be breaking down.

In this chapter, my story unfolds, completely and honestly, including the highs *and* lows. You see, even with a business degree and background in creating financial software, I was shocked by the hard lessons I encountered on my path. It was a tough realization to accept that the pressures of running a large corporation just did not compare to, or prepare me for, the monumental demands of starting my own small company; the experiences were worlds apart. My hope is for my story to encourage you to keep going, no matter where on the journey you currently find yourself; I hope you'll learn from each step along the path as I did. Ultimately, my journey led to discoveries about myself, my beliefs, and my values, but mostly I discovered my indominable strength and faith in my abilities when faced with crushing failures. This is *also* a story of forgiveness and grace, two salves I poured over myself to recover and *get up* after tough business lessons knocked me down. It is my goal (and, I hope, yours) to use each failure as a learning tool towards success and to celebrate the lessons that have moved me closer and closer to my goals. I invite you to learn with me and embrace my mantra, *just keep going.*

My story began in the year 2000 when I started my first business in the interior design industry to offer custom window treatments to homeowners. Like many in the industry, I did not come in with a big plan to make lots of money, nor did I have a big plan for processes and procedures (where was LuAnn's first book eighteen years ago?!). My foray into self-employment began because I had a talent and skill to offer as a service to others. Never mind that pricing custom work was foreign to me! At the time, I did not know a single person offering this service, so there was no one to ask. I just made purchases at retail and then resold as part of a completed project. Half the time I used a coupon *and passed along all discounts to my client!* I never charged for all the time involved in their project whether it was designing, shopping, planning, or sewing; I only charged for a small portion of my time while sewing. There were so many profit-defeating choices I made without even a shred of awareness.

Sometimes these oversights happen as a byproduct of being new to the work, and sometimes they happen from jumping in too quickly without any forethought. I had a healthy dose of both. Now, let's fast forward—tax season came along.

Up to this point in my story, I had already jumped in and had begun to plow ahead without a financial plan. Neither did I purchase an accounting system. Remember, my background was in financial software, and I knew how to allocate and account for funds—so I created an Excel spreadsheet! I did this at the end of March, for the prior year. (You can see that on-time accounting was *not* a priority!)

My Excel spreadsheet revealed my first startling discovery from that first year: I could sell, but I was not profitable. The numbers showed money coming in, but not enough money to spend after all supplies and business expenses were removed. My internal voice shrieked, "Whaaat?!" Forget profit, I had not even been paid a salary! Nevertheless, I convinced myself it was fine since I fulfilled a higher purpose; "You love what you do and people are so thankful." Have you ever told yourself a story to make your poor decision-making sound less ominous? Then, I did it all again for *another* year, the same way, but with a *few* tweaks.

This time, when I used coupons to purchase at retail, I did not pass along the savings. I also realized the need to charge for more than the sewing. Better, but still not a profitable *strategy*. Unfortunately, I did not focus on my financials and monthly reconciliations and accounting. I just *assumed* that everything would work out at the end of the year. It's painful to see that in print; I'm shaking my head now, and it might seem obvious that this is flawed logic. But I had to discover that, for all my practical financial skills, I felt blocked and reluctant to apply them. Luckily, I stopped neglecting and began to pay attention to my financials. This became one of my best lessons from this time: be disciplined to keep up with your financials monthly *at a minimum* and remember that making great sales numbers does not equate to profitability. **Note:** I purposely describe the process as one to "keep up with," not one to understand. You will see what I mean in a bit.

At about year three, my pattern of profitability had not really improved even though my income had. I felt disgusted with myself and knew there had to be a course correction. Otherwise, I would go back to working a corporate job, which I did not want to do. I had a heart-to-heart with myself. Similar to the exercises LuAnn takes you through, first I decided that no matter what, I would own my business, every choice and decision. Next, I wrote down what it meant to be in a business instead of a hobby. Whoa! When I looked honestly at my business, I realized that some of my actions were those of a hobbyist and not a business entrepreneur. Here are a few examples: I did not set scheduled work time. My jobs came with no terms and conditions, nor any defined process from beginning to end. I was letting myself be taken advantage of. I analyzed the weaknesses from this list, and I decided to improve these areas so that profit would follow. This is when I got real with myself, my business, my ideal client, my processes and procedures. I updated my business name, changed the type of business from sole proprietor to LLC, and got a resale certificate. No way was I going to continue in the same path, no matter how happy my clients were, because I was miserable.

Here is the resulting list that shaped the next phase of my business:

Plan to Profit

1. Make a choice to be profitable.
2. Do an honest business assessment looking at all areas.
3. Change the activities that are not leading you to profitability.
4. Make peace with your decisions and move forward.

One area on which I focused most was pricing my custom offerings. *That* could be a whole other book, but I will share this nugget: I had to price each item for profit. My business was too small to have multiple loss leaders. My time was too precious. I had to make peace with my pricing. Often, I could not afford my work, and neither could my friends. But I was in a luxury market and luxury prices come with that. I truly believe that confidence comes with making peace with our offerings, our client, and our value. When you know that you can deliver what you promise with great service, then you feel better about pricing. None of this happened overnight, and yes, there were sweaty palms when I handed out a few invoices. But once one person paid, I had confidence giving out the invoice to the second. This created one of my new rules to live by: If two people are willing to pay my price, the market can handle it. *Keep going.*

At this point, I had this whole business thing down and started being able to pay myself and cover the bills. Hello financial freedom! But hold on, did I hear the sound of brakes squealing? The net profit at the bottom of my income statement was not enough to cover the salary that I wanted and the profit I needed to run my company without putting my *own* money back in as a loan. My husband sweetly called himself my angel investor during those years. That's a humbling feeling, or mortifying.

I had to really make peace again with the fact that I was not stupid. Yes, that sounds harsh. But when we know something and take our eye off that element to focus somewhere else, the judge and jury take up residence in our brain and call us guilty immediately. There's an emotional component to failure that makes us feel ashamed, and I had to struggle against that feeling with some grace and forgiveness. I *did* know the reason, solution, and path forward. Simply, I had never set up a salary goal and a profit goal separately. Duh! In corporate this would have made sense, but for some reason it did not occur to me as an LLC that all the money at the bottom of my income statement needed to cover more than my bring-home pay. I had to forgive myself for forgetting this and allow myself the grace to get up, moving ahead armed with the knowledge *now*. Maybe you are in a similar situation. If so, chin up. You can do this! Here is the plan that I used to move forward:

Plan to Profit

1. Determine the salary I want to make.
2. Determine how much profit I needed to make for the company.
3. Adjust processes and procedures.
4. Review prices to make sure they are in alignment with my goals.

At this point, my journey was going well, and my business took off. My salary jumped to where I wanted it to be and I thought it was all chocolate and roses, until that darn April rolled around again and taxes were due. I completed our family taxes, and we had a huge amount due to both federal and state. I felt physically ill. Why did that happen? Where did that tax bill come from? Where was I going to get the money?

With profitability comes tax payments. In my haste to celebrate my newfound financial freedom, I had not saved properly for taxes. This represents another lesson learned the hard way. My HR department had fallen down on the job (that was me). Again, as an LLC, net income was more than only salary and profit: it was before-tax salary. Now, I wasn't just feeling bad, but also extremely frustrated. Good grief, would the financial lessons ever be over? Once again, I stood back up and brushed myself off. My family found a way to make that tax payment, and I vowed at that moment that *never* again would I be ignorant of the amount I owed in taxes. *Never* again would I bring money into my home to spend and not have some saved back. *Never* again would I want to feel robbed of joy at a year well done because I did not consider the tax burden of success. I discovered my resiliency and my ability to harness my resolve.

There is another way to think about taxes, but I cannot disagree more with it. Some of you may ascribe to a theory that I heard repeatedly, which is earn less to avoid paying taxes. That just seemed crazy to me. I was in build mode, not hold-back mode. If I was not in business to make money, I should just go do volunteer work. Enter in the next moment of grace and forgiveness: I had to make peace with taxes as a proxy for success and to forgive myself yet again for not thinking about this. It was just a fact to accept that more income brings more taxes.

In the end, I discovered the importance of help from professionals and the value of informed financial decisions. I had a great accountant who helped me find ways to avoid taxes—legally, of course! She also helped with buying decisions based on my income. Fortunately, I was flush with resources, and I had only to apply them appropriately. Trust me in this: your accountant hates bearing the bad news that you owe a huge amount of money for which you didn't allocate just as much as you'll hate hearing it. They dread the discussion; there is no delight. To recover from this low point, here are the steps I took next:

Plan to Profit

1. Identify the personal income taxes due for federal and state based on my situation.
2. Create a bank account to move money into for tax payments.
3. Move to quarterly estimated taxes instead of waiting to pay once a year.

Lessons learned, right? Back to financial freedom and a booming business, right? Wrong. Nothing is usually that simple in business. My journey of discovery continued. After a few years of paying myself a salary and paying taxes with no issue, my income took another leap forward. This time my accountant strongly suggested in *March* that I should put some money into an IRA account to save for the future and to reduce the tax burden. This idea was super exciting to me, yet I felt a twinge of self-recrimination, like when I did not have money for taxes when they came due, because I had not saved individually for tax retirement. Subsequently, that net income had to be parsed out *again!* I felt awful that I was unable to put the entire amount for which I was eligible by law into an IRA because *I just did not have it*. But this experience provided another turning point for me. My goal was to avoid reducing my bring-home salary because my family relied on that. Instead, I saw that the only way to add money into retirement was to make *more* and save it separately from my profit. At that time, the profit was being used to reinvest back into my business and to allow for some extra family fun like a trip to Jamaica. I readjusted and here was the plan I formed:

Plan for Profit

1. Determine how much profit needed to stay in the company.
2. Determine how much I wanted to save for retirement.
3. Move the money into another bank account to save.

As my business continued to grow and change, it became apparent that I needed to save for other items. Herein lay another step on my path that required forgiveness: I was caught off-guard by retirement savings despite my previous knowledge. Foremost, my upbringing included training in fiscal responsibility. My parents raised us to save/spend our money as follows: we gave ten percent to tithe or charity, twenty percent to savings, and seventy percent was ours to spend. (We were too young for the tax discussion.) We even had a triple-divided piggy bank! As a result, creating two or three bank accounts was nothing new to me. In addition, at the beginning of our marriage, my husband and I took a financial management class at our church. This was even before Dave Ramsey. Although, I was well-equipped with good financial values, despite all these qualifications and my formal education, I still had a missing link when it came to managing my business finances.

Instead of going to the bank and opening new bank accounts as I was wont to do, I veered from my tried-and-true habits and tried a spreadsheet to allocate the money in my main checking account. This was a perfect idea, in theory. In practice, this idea did *not* work. The spreadsheet was only as good as my ability to maintain it. My maintenance was spotty; some months, I kept up, but too many other months, it was neglected. The result was an untrustworthy document that became useless. Even though I knew what I wanted to accomplish, my plan would not get me there because the process itself was a bit cumbersome. It was a pretty good plan, but not a *fantastic* plan; "pretty good" would not result in the profitability I desired.

Then I made the game-changing discovery that launched my journey into overdrive. In 2015, a coaching client mentioned a book she had read that seemed as though it was written by me. "It sounds *just* like you!" she said, recognizing the same analogies that I use. Weird. Cool. I needed to check this out! Thank goodness for Amazon Prime because I had that book in my hands and devoured by the next day. I had discovered *Profit First* by Mike Michalowicz.

My reaction was swift and represented another major turning point. Upon finishing the book, I emailed Profit First (PF) headquarters immediately and said I needed to speak with someone. A member jumped on the phone with me, and I shared about the similar methods I taught to my clients. I confessed that my fatal flaw was running it all by spreadsheet, because a document for financial data makes it too easy to twist around the numbers, feel frustrated, and give up, as was my experience. Through PF, I discovered the answer to tracking all the numbers: no more spreadsheet at all! PF is an elegant and brilliant process. And it worked. That was it! I was sold on the process that had finally filled in the blanks of the system I had been using. That day, I joined the PF Family and started the work to become a Profit First Certified Coach. Immediately, I made changes in my own business and then created Master Your Profit, an online course for my clients to teach them how to apply Profit First directly for the interior design industry. My relationship with PF ushered in a new era for my business and for me.

What is Profit First? It is a money management system that uses our natural tendency to look at our bank accounts for information to make business decisions. PF also recognizes entrepreneurial poverty as a real problem and creates strategies to reduce this tendency. In the

PF world, profit is removed from sales and expenses are the leftover. In the accounting world, expenses are removed from sales and profit is the leftover. By learning to take our profit first, we force the company to survive within its means. This was huge! My journey just took a permanent detour and cruised toward profitability.

With my new-found Profit First understanding, here were my next steps in managing my profit:

Plan for Profit

1. Open all the bank accounts I wanted and needed. This meant no more spreadsheet monitoring.
2. Make a plan to allocate my funds consistently and put reminders in my calendar.
3. Review all of my expenses to cut any excess so that my company could live within its means.
4. Review pricing and process and procedures again and again.

As we return to my story, I would like to say it ends with, "Whew, I have arrived! Done." Truly, my business methods improved, and I was super excited about the impact I saw merely by thinking differently. The thought process of taking my profit first allowed me to create major changes. However, as I shared my new knowledge with my clients and they began implementing Profit First, it quickly became apparent that there was a big divide between depositing money into a bank account and fully understanding the financial documents of a company. PF was never meant to be a stand-alone behavior but rather a fully integrated strategy to coordinate with your financial statements. You still need bookkeepers and accountants (and I daresay coaches) to help guide you toward financial health. To really get great at PF, we must be able to see where the money is going in our company. Here is what I taught my clients in the Understanding Your Financials course:

Plan to and for Profit

1. Become familiar with the Income Statement and Balance Sheet.
2. Create a company budget and let the company live on that.
3. Create a financial plan and goals to make the plan happen.
4. Monitor your financials and have a plan to do this regularly.
5. Understand where your company numbers translate to your taxes.
6. Give oversight to any financial preparations completed by your accountant and bookkeeper.
7. Make sure you are delivering the right product/service to the right client at the right price and then manage the money.
8. Stay the course. Adjust frequently as needed.

Now here I am, nineteen years after I opened my doors to begin my journey in the interior design world. As they say, I have come a long way, baby! I will not say that this concludes my story, because growth and discovery are constants (and should be!). However, the page turns on that chapter, and I am happy to be in the next part of my journey that includes wisdom from hindsight and confidence from experience. Being in business is not easy. It takes dedication and commitment to your craft and to the areas of your company that are not in your wheelhouse.

As you look back, I am sure you have come a long way, too! There will be trip-ups and falls, and maybe some scraped knees. *Always get up.* There are times you will celebrate the successes large and small, but there *will* be times when you will cry with embarrassment. These are all part of the process. Each of these moments guide us towards doing business better. I stand as a testament to the fact that if you don't price properly or manage the money in your business properly, you will become jaded, depressed, uncaring and ultimately want to quit. That is not what I want for you or for me.

We have now turned full circle in my story and come back to the beginning. Profit is a choice. It must be planned for and managed. It is necessary to stay in business and to grow. You will sleep better at night when you are profitable. Take the time to focus on the financial health of your business at the same level that you focus on the marketing or execution of your design work. It is like a three-legged stool: market for clients, deliver the product, and make and manage your income. No way can a business stay up with only two legs! Until you get all three parts of your business going strong, you may take some tumbles and get some bruises. Just. Keep. Going.

Read and repeat after me:

> *It is possible to be creative and to be in charge of my money. I take full and complete responsibility as the owner and leader of my business to be profitable.*

This is essential to your success. Please never underestimate your ability to achieve it.

I love Michele's observation and her challenge question to us: "Have you ever told yourself a story to make your poor decision-making sound less ominous?"

It makes you think, doesn't it? Does it also make you cringe? The truth is that since we are creative, maybe the finance side of our business doesn't come as intuitively as the design side does, but that is no excuse.

Take Michele's lessons and advice to heart. Don't run from them. Don't tell yourself a story to make yourself feel better. You and I both know you won't ultimately feel better by telling yourself stories anyway. You must take control of your business by planning for profit.

The great news is that, through her journey, you can avoid experiencing some of her hard-earned lessons firsthand, because Michele is here to cut you to the front of the line. If this is an area where you struggle, I suggest you listen to her podcast Profit Is a Choice for more lessons, insights and advice.

Prepare yourself to be encouraged, to be inspired, and to be empowered to run your business profitably. After all, you are running a business, not a hobby, right?
- LN

About the Author

Michele Williams is the owner of Scarlet Thread Consulting. Using her software development and interior design business background, she empowers her clients to charge what they are worth and to have confidence in their financials. Michele is a Profit First-certified coach focused on the interior design industry, and she hosts the popular podcast *Profit Is a Choice*.

Michele has appeared on LuAnn's podcast three times, on episodes 137, 180, and 395:

https://luannnigara.com/137-michele-williams-scarlet-thread-consulting-actionable-tips-for-time-management/

https://luannnigara.com/180-power-talk-friday-michele-williams-talks-about-profit-first-and-why-it-matters-to-you/

https://luannnigara.com/395-power-talk-friday-michele-williams-financial-health-checklist-for-your-interior-design-business/

CHAPTER 4

Nancy Ganzekaufer

N ancy burst into my world the very first month I launched the podcast. Like many of the other coaches I would come to meet in the next few years, Nancy was recommended to me. We hopped on a call, and as I began to explain my goal and my "why" for the podcast, she started blowing my mind right then and there. Her mind raced with topics we could cover teaching and inspiring interior designers to run their businesses more intentionally, always with the end goal of creating more revenue and being more profitable.

Nancy is from New York and I'm a Jersey girl. We're both fast talkers, laugh easily, and are passionate about business, sales in particular. With all that mixed together, we found instant chemistry. Our mutual respect started during that first phone call and has grown exponentially from there. We have done several collaborations since then. This book is another, and I know it won't be our last. When I find a like-minded, no nonsense, #smartlady, I hang on. Nancy is all of that and more.

Nancy has appeared in four episodes as of this writing. Each has been a what I call a "pen and paper" episode: the kind of show that you might be listening to while driving or exercising, but ten minutes in, you know you are going to have to listen again, this time with pen and paper.

In her chapter, Nancy talks about charging what you are worth for your services. This is one of the most common and toughest challenges we face as business coaches, namely helping you see you. Helping you see and *own your value, and helping you gain the confidence you deserve that sets you up to be a successful, profitable business owner. Nancy is excellent at this. She has the right mix of "kick you in the butt" and "let's regroup; it will be okay."*

See if you agree with me.

- LN

The Confidence to Charge Your Worth
By Nancy Ganzekaufer

I'm just going to say it. I give you permission to charge what you are worth. It's time!

Charging what you are worth is one of the hardest things that interior designers and all service-based entrepreneurs face. Knowing your value and having the guts to charge for it takes work, introspection, and confidence. As a business coach to interior designers and other creatives, I can tell you that ninety-eight percent of my clients are not charging enough for their services when they first come to me.

Here are some reasons you may not be charging what you are worth:

- You don't think you would ever pay for the service you provide to others.
- You don't run your business like a business; you run it like a hobby. You go haphazardly from client to client without a distinct process to follow and you think it shows.
- You were taught from an early age that money doesn't grow on trees. You put yourself in the shoes of your clients rather than calculate the worth of your service.
- You get sucked into your client's money story, namely that they are hemorrhaging money and have to be careful.
- You never learned the words to use to show value and sell to your clients. Sales scare you.

- You are not confident enough in your company's processes and service experience to charge what you are worth.
- You worry that you won't get the job and you desperately need the money. So, you undercharge, thinking that it will help you get the job.

What I'm going to teach you in this chapter are just some of the ways that I learned to not only appear confident, but to be truly confident enough to charge what you need in order to run a profitable business, a business that brings you joy and the client excellent results.

Have you experienced one or more of the following situations?

- You get notice that a designer market is coming up and you want to go, but you don't have the money in your business account to spend.
- You feel as though you would like to hire your first assistant or another employee, but you are scared that your business cashflow can't handle it.
- You see a great training that you want to take or a coach that you know can help you grow in profitability, but you are waiting until you can afford it.
- You've dreamed of having a studio outside your home and just can't seem to make it a reality, because money is tight and you don't know where your next dollar is coming from.
- You are not able to pay your bills.

What I want for you is to have enough confidence to charge more and face tough challenges so that you don't have to hesitate when you see an opportunity to invest in your business, invest in yourself, or pay your bills. We all deserve to get paid what we are worth based on the results we provide, and you are no exception.

Don't get me wrong: I still suffer from lack of confidence whenever I stretch myself towards a new goal. When doing something that is new and outside your comfort zone, you can expect some nerves. All I ask is that you stay with me and use the techniques I'm about to share with you and watch your confidence and bank account grow.

Whenever I try something new in my business or in my personal life, the nasty little voice of doubt peeks in, saying that I may not be good enough or organized enough or that I'm going to look stupid. Together, we will fight all that self-doubt and kick its ass. You can do it.

Root Systems Destroying Self-Confidence

I have become aware of root systems in play here over the years. Our lack of self-confidence doesn't just come out of nowhere. It may start at a young age so subtly that when we get older, we cannot track where it began.

Before I get into some exercises to help you feel more confident in both your business pricing and with customer interactions, I would like to highlight two root systems that may be cultivating a lack of self-confidence in your life.

I would like to put out a challenge to all of you. Be open to discovering other rooted issues or systems in your life that don't empower you to grow and develop greater confidence. Sometimes our culture likes to get around introspection or taking a real good look at ourselves and the environments surrounding us, because that might mean change needs to happen. Change is not always comfortable, but those needed changes are what helps to set up a more prosperous and dynamic future, far beyond what you can see right now.

Doing this introspective work can really trip us up because we uncover and discover where we actually stand, and it can be scary. Then we need to decide how to best move our lives and businesses towards a better place.

With that, let's look at the two potential root systems that could be affecting you.

1. Conditioned to Be Overly Accommodating and Subservient

Many of us have been groomed to believe that we must be overly accommodating. Our culture over many decades has taught us that we must be overly gracious, overly apologetic, and subservient in order to please others at all costs and make everyone feel comfortable.

While this might be a short-term way of appeasing people, it is detrimental to your long-term self-confidence and business. It short-circuits the level at which you can be productive, because you are afraid to lead and direct a situation or act as the expert and shine. However, one thing that I've found when you "arise and shine" is that your new behavior naturally filters out people and opportunities that no longer match where you are, and more of what brings you abundance starts to show up.

When you reflect, has this root system of being overly pleasing and accommodating penetrated your heart and mind? Do you find yourself feeling guilty for wanting to be more assertive and asking for more of what you need and desire to have a flourishing business and personal life?

2. Being Pushed out of the Game

We all have noticed over the last decade that technology and/or a younger generation may be trying to replace us and our skill, to make it appear that we are not needed anymore. How can that not do a number on someone's self-confidence? Even if that scenario hasn't happened to you, enough of it is happening around us to create some fear and guessing on our end.

The good news is that this phenomenon seems to be working back toward our favor. Educating clients on exactly what you do for them is imperative to counterbalance technology and the age of internet shopping and do-it-yourselfers. There is nothing like a seasoned professional with all the industry skills, education, connections, communication skills, track record, and professionalism. The world needs what you have! Now it's your turn to learn the skills it takes to deliver a confident message about your value.

This is a time for you to reinvent yourself for the expert that you are, because there will always be a void to fill in this industry. What you have is needed and will definitely be requested. You just need to present yourself with distinction and self-confidence.

I know there are more root systems, but I find these two to be very prevalent but yet, not something we are always aware of as ingredients to the low self-confidence we can sometimes have.

Now that the groundwork has been laid, let's focus on the practical ways to boost self-confidence.

Confidence-Boosting Exercises

Write down in excruciating detail what you can do in the world of interior design for a client. Break it down into four sections.

1. List all the education, experience, and awards you have in the industry.

Make sure you include all your trips to market, what you learned, your continuing education, and seminars you've done related to interior design. Do this even if you're a new interior designer. You got into this business for a reason and you need to write down what makes you ready. Have you designed your own home, a friend's home, or, most commonly, a family member's home? Write that down.

If you don't have much to talk about, create something to talk about. I am sure you can help a handful of people in your life in order to build up your portfolio and confidence. Treat these projects as if they were your high-paying clients. This will help you get your feet wet in a "safe place."

2. Spell out everything you can do for a client in an initial consultation.

Write out everything you can do for a client in an initial paid consultation. Yes, it should be paid! For example, in one and a half to two hours, what can you accomplish for a client that will save them time, money, and mistakes moving forward? Will you help them pick paint colors? Will you help them figure out what window treatments would be best for their space? Can you help them decide on how a room can be reconfigured to make it more useful and appealing? Can you provide initial thoughts and suggestions on hard surfaces, lighting, flooring, tile, built-ins, and so on?

List everything you can think of that you have helped somebody with in the past on an initial consultation or anything you know you're capable of helping them with at that first in-person meeting.

3. Outline all that you do in the design phase.

This is the stage that most clients don't understand at all. You become a design therapist, friend, educator, and creator of amazing design based on their space, needs, and personality. This is not an easy task! It is worth a lot. I know you see it and know it, but how do you make the client understand?

Write it all down. What happens in the design phase? This will help you feel your value and explain it to a client when challenged. You may create floor plans, elevations, select finishes, fabrics, design window treatments, select all furnishings, appliances, lighting, accessories, and artwork, among other things. Review and keep files up to date so nothing is missed. You meet with vendors and reps; take your own measurements and verify service provider measurements; select soft materials and hard finishes; and communicate all selections and decisions with the vendors, workmen, and contractors so they can calculate estimates for you. Then you put together all the estimates, including your margins for the client presentation, and create client presentations within their anticipated investment amount!

Next, add some unknowns, such as finding new vendors and suppliers, creating relationships with them, learning about the quality of their work or products, setting up accounts, and ensuring that you understand their process.

All of these areas encompass your expertise and provide a huge value to a client. You need to be prepared to explain what your profession entails if you are questioned about your pricing.

Don't forget you also create a physical or virtual mood board with samples, meet with the client again, negotiate changes, and go back and find a new selection for one or two items.

What else do you do? Write it all down right now.

This includes getting bids/estimates, getting pricing on custom pieces, pricing window treatments, pillows, art, flooring, and other décor elements. You order and wait for samples, and you correspond with vendors and reps during this process. You check on availability, lead times, and freight.

4. Write down everything that happens in the procurement stage.

The procurement stage is when you start ordering everything you selected for the client.

It involves everything from meeting with company reps and showrooms; carefully ordering the right size, shape, and color for all products; followed by creating purchase orders and placing orders; managing phone calls, clarifications, and payment to vendors, workrooms, and contractors; tracking and following up on all items ordered; managing the receiver and/or delivery to final location with installation; coordinating additional installations, such as window treatments, art installation, and so on; creating a remaining punch list and a game plan for any damages; and managing placement, staging, and styling of all deliverables for the big reveal and for photo day. Don't forget last-minute local shopping for finishing touches.

All of this is within your company's responsibility. All of this is a potential liability to you!

The first step is for you to list all these things out in your own handwriting, in your own words, so that you start to feel all the value that you bring and all the time, frustration, and money you save your clients. You want to write down everything so that you highlight your value, creativity and talent for interior design, from the "simpler" tasks to the detailed and complicated amazing vision.

Let's talk about your vendors, trusted advisors, contractors and workers. Who do you want on your team for these projects? Who have you learned to trust on previous projects? Have you found over the years a great painter? A great wallpaper person? An amazing plumber, tile installer, cabinet maker, workroom, or handyperson? All these people are a part of your business arsenal. This is of great value to a client.

Even if you're still finding them and expanding your team, this gives potential clients even more reason to hire you. You've got trusted options. These are just some more reasons why you are valuable. Make a list of them, too: your team, your subcontractors, and your trusted advisors. When you're calculating how much you're worth and trying to gain confidence to charge more, read these lists and understand what you actually bring to the table.

Can I get a "hell yeah, I'm worth it!"?

Banish the Idea of "Competition"

I don't believe in the word competition.

Here's why.

Your ideal client will be attracted to you for who you are, the professionalism of your company, the systems you've put into place, and what they believe is the talent that you bring to the table. Someone who is not your ideal client won't relate to your branding, the way you carry yourself, or the words you use. This is why it's so important to always be yourself, because if you try to model yourself after another interior designer or business owner, it will not be sustainable, make you happy, or attract your ideal client.

I equate this to dating. If you are trying so hard to be someone you think your date wants and not who you really are in the beginning, the relationship is doomed to fail. Be the best version of yourself from the start, and they'll always know what to expect!

Let your audience see your unique way of doing things, because creativity is a boundless and abundant well that doesn't run dry. How you can structure your services and interactions to be done in a way that turns heads and has people saying, "I have not quite seen it done like that before, but I like it"?

Your value includes not only your time working on a client's project, but it also includes your creative eye and skill, your past education, your continuing education, and all that it takes to run a top-notch business providing availability, excellent service, and an amazing end result.

There is no glory in being the cheapest in your market. There's no glory in being in the middle of the pack either. The glory comes when you are the premier option in your market with a process, experience, and end results for your client that are exemplary. If your results and service level match your prices, you will be golden.

How do you get confident enough to raise your prices? Making a list of everything you can do at each step of the design process is one way. Making a list of your team of advisors is another way. You can also present or highlight your testimonials and the positive emails you've gotten over the years for your service.

What now? How do you find the confidence to tell new potential clients what your upgraded fees are? It's going to sound simple but here it is; just dive into it!

Before sending a new proposal with your new fees or before you get on the phone, read your own past testimonials, emails, and reviews that you've gotten about your service. Really feel the words people have said. Ask yourself, "Am I good at what I do?" If the answer is yes, then it's time to feel your worth and ask for what you are worth.

Allow yourself to look at your talent as others see it. You don't have to be humble in this moment. This moment you are working on increasing your confidence to charge what you are worth. Write it down, read it, and feel it!

Let your potential clients see what organizations you are a part of and what notable clients have requested your services or consultation. Show a charted comparison of the value you add to your services, in comparison to what it is more typical and expected in this field. Show off the ways you go the extra mile for individual clients.

After that, what I want you to do is look them in the eye or sit tall while talking on the phone and tell them your fee without hesitation! Then breathe, pause, and let them respond. You will be surprised how silence relays confidence. Babbling and filling the silence relays insecurity.

No Apologies, Just Fix It!

This section really speaks to who you are as a company. I firmly believe that if you are confident in your ability to handle mishaps, you will be confident charging what you are worth.

Always face a client who is upset with you, your company, or part of the process right away. Do not run away or delay responding to an issue that comes up. Deal with it head on and swiftly.

You want to make it right without apologizing for an issue that was not within your control. People want action more than words! In a number of cases, apologizing sheepishly can undermine your authority and legitimacy. However, if you are assertive, polite, professional, and action-oriented and dive into executing the solution, you will gain more respect and trust with your clients.

The truth is, something is going to go wrong at some point. There is no way to get around it. Would you rather take the weak stance and sheepishly apologize or the strong stance and get into fix-it mode? You might have to muster up a bit more courage from time to time, but it is well worth the trust and reputation that you build with clients along the way.

Here's a sample response to a client who is upset when her lighting doesn't arrive in time for her party. "Hi Mary, Unfortunately, the shipment of your custom pendant lights for your kitchen is delayed. As disappointing as that is, we are tracking their progress and when they get here, they will be amazing. Patience can be difficult in these situations, but we can set up an interim plan for lighting in the kitchen prior to your party. Let's talk tomorrow on the phone and make a plan."

Here, I addressed the client's emotions but did not apologize for something that was not within my control. Notice how I downplayed the drama the client might be feeling and stayed logical and professional.

It takes practice and patience to explain things and not run away from them when times get tough. We all know things can go wrong with all size projects and you must practice being calm and professional.

Another example that you may need to work on is gaining the confidence to face a client to tell them that the additional items or advice they are asking you for is outside of the scope of the original project and you'll need to charge extra. This is often called "scope creep." You all have heard it: "While you are looking for that lamp for my living room, can you also see if you can find accessories for my master bedroom?"

As a business owner, it's a necessary evil that you must deal with on a regular basis. When you gain confidence on what words to use for each uncomfortable money conversation, these talks get easier. This will change your enjoyment of your job and increase your profitability. Let me lay out some scenarios for you.

Scenario number one: A client tells you they really like you, but your pricing is just too high. What do you do?

You say, "I understand that you feel that way. Let me ask you first, did I accurately outline the scope of the project correctly? Okay, good. I'd like you to know something about me; I'm really good at what I do. Your project will have a stellar outcome when you use me (my company)."

Client: "You are more expensive than others."

You: "That may be, although I personally don't keep track of others' prices. All I know is that when you hire me, you get the best service, selections, and outcomes. My team of industry partners are top-notch. You won't be disappointed."

You: "Ready to do this?" :)

If they are still not prepared to move forward, you can offer a different service level if you have one, which I highly recommend you do.

Do not compromise the profitability of your company or of a particular job by negotiating your rates. Once you have figured out what you need to be a profitable company, you need to stick to it. Don't get sucked into a client's money story or their mindset of scarcity.

Offer a lesser, modified service so they can get time to work with you further. Then, perhaps, work your way up to full service when they are left with too much of the ordering, tracking, and problem solving for their liking. This is all within your control. You are the owner of your company and you can make another offer, or you do have the option of walking away professionally with a "thank you and I'm here if you ever need me."

Mindset Shift Exercises

Now that you've written down who you are, what you do, and why you deserve to charge what you're worth, on paper you look like the most awesome interior decorator rock star on the planet. By the looks of things, anyone who needs your services should just drop the check for you on your doorstep!

Even with all this excellence in front of your face, you might still be having confidence issues. Your emotions might not line up with all that's on paper. That's okay, and it is curable.

1. Get some paper and start writing down all the negative thoughts and feelings you are having. Be as detailed and accurate as you can. Do not try to downplay how you feel. Once you have written everything down, read it over. Then, rip it into shreds, throw it in the trash can, and don't look back. This signals to our minds that those thoughts have been evicted and we are not tolerating those thoughts anymore.

2. Get your journal. Write the truly positive things you feel that you would like to believe in more and be reminded of. Just write everything good down, even if it doesn't relate to your business. Just bolster your world with positive thoughts, such as I love that I get to cultivate my own life, I am really good at what I do, people are drawn to my smile and generosity, and there is so much abundance that I will always have what I need.

3. Listen to affirmations while you fall asleep. Sometimes we obsess over changing and shifting mindsets to the point that it becomes an even bigger problem. However, when you are listening to affirmations as you fall asleep, you are changing your mind without strenuous effort. Before you know it, you will suddenly seem to have a more positive outlook on everything around you, giving you that extra boost of confidence for your business. You can buy affirmation mp3's online or listen to them on YouTube. My favorite mantra is "Make it easy." I learned that from one of my first coaches years ago and it still works for me when I'm fighting myself and struggling with trying something new. Perhaps it will work for you too.

4. Leave the doubters in the dark. The last thing you need are the voices of those who nag you with disbelief. It is more than enough to contend with your own negativity, but adding more

from outside voices will only make it harder. To shift mindsets, you must keep the negative out.

Just keep practicing. You have to be willing to reinforce the truth about yourself, your business, your goals, and your relationships. The mind is a muscle and you have to build it up in the way you want it to go!

Go forth and charge what you are worth. There's really no other way.

Remember that confidence is a brand that sells.

Guess what my favorite line in the entire chapter is? "Don't get sucked into your client's money story."

Read it again: "Don't get sucked into your client's money story."

If your client cannot afford the sofa and the rug, guess what, they have to make a choice. If they cannot afford to redo the kitchen and the bathroom, they have to make a choice. You are not their bank and you are not their mother. Grown-ups decide what they can afford, and they also go without what they cannot afford. If the chandelier is so perfect and they simply must have it, it's up to them to figure out how to afford it. It is not your job to lower the price or to lower your fees. It is your responsibility to offer a suitable alternative within their budget but then they decide which one to buy.

Do you personally ever expect any service provider or establishment you patronize to lower the price to fit the budget you had in mind?

"Oh waiter, I see the fish special is $34.00, but when I add in the bottle of wine at $40, I will be over my dinner budget by $14.00. Oh, but the fish sounds really delicious, you can just give it all to me for $60.00, right?"

"Miss Hairdresser, I really need a cut and color today but that is over my budget, can you just throw in the haircut? I mean it's only $50, and I'm a really good client of yours."

It quite literally sounds ridiculous, doesn't it? So, why do you think you have to make an adjustment when you hear: "I love the $10,000 rug, it is so much nicer than the $8000 one. Can't you just sell me the $10,000 one for $8000? I have so much more work to do with you, can't you make this work?"

You cannot imagine anyone thinking a hairdresser should work for free or a waiter lowering the price of a meal, so why in the world should anyone think you would take hundreds or thousands off of the price of goods or deduct from your billable hours? The better question is, why would you?

My great hope is that if you struggle with charging your worth that you will reread Nancy's chapter as often as you need to. Whenever you feel a bit pressured or unsure, pull the book off the shelf and let Nancy give you the kick in the butt along with the gentle reassurance you need in order to value yourself, your talents, and your services for every penny they are worth.

- LN

About the Author

Nancy Ganzekaufer is a focused, motivated, and dedicated interior designer business coach. As a mom of three young adults and a successful business owner, Nancy understands the unique challenges entrepreneurs face when pursuing their dreams of growing a profitable business. She leads by example through her hard work, encouragement, and most of all, her no-BS leadership style.

Nancy has appeared on LuAnn's podcast four times, on episodes 15, 159, 256, and 389:

https://luannnigara.com/15-nancy-ganzekaufer-niche-is-rich/

https://luannnigara.com/159-power-talk-friday-nancy-ganzekaufer-how-to-get-confident-clear-on-what-you-offer/

https://luannnigara.com/256-nancy-ganzekaufer-a-powerful-strategy-to-attract-more-clients/

https://luannnigara.com/389-power-talk-friday-nancy-ganzekaufer-the-interior-design-profit-formula/

Section Two

Operations, the Daily

CHAPTER 5

Sarah Daniele

*S*arah Daniele is a process and systems lady. As you will learn in this chapter, beginning with a drive to organize and better manage her own interior design firm, she ultimately created Mydoma Studio to help you do exactly that in your firm.

Since meeting Sarah in 2016, I have come to admire many things about her in addition to her organized approach to her business. For one, I love that she saw a need in the marketplace and went for it. So often, we have an idea for a product or a service and that's the end of it. We decide, "No one will want this, it's too expensive to create, and it'll take too long to build," and so it remains a half-baked idea on the back burner. Not Sarah, no way. She believed in her idea and her ability to create it. With the help of her husband Tom, they have designed an intuitive, efficient platform for running your business productively, enabling you to be more profitable. I love that.

Two more things I have come to love about Sarah are her integrity, and her passion for helping her team, her clients, and industry partners achieve their goals. Both Sarah's head and her heart are in the right place. You can count on that.

As you read this chapter, let her words sink in. Think about how you are currently running your firm. Do you have room for improvement? Could you or should you tweak your processes?

I want to point out something to notice as you read her chapter. Sarah makes the case for having systems and she suggests ideas for them, but she also asks you to notice if there is any part of your current process that isn't working. Similarly, I encourage designers to do an autopsy at the end of every project. Sit down and go through every phase. Were there any missteps? Were there any conflicts with the client or any of the vendors? Next, brainstorm on how they could have been avoided. Do you need to revise a current system or implement a new one? Ask yourself what could have been different? And here's a hint—every answer begins with: "If I had done this, then this would have happened, so next time I'll ..."

You are responsible for every single thing in your firm, good and bad. When you analyze the problems honestly, you will always find that you personally could have done something different to create a better outcome.

It all begins with a finite, duplicatable process, because this eliminates the on-the-fly decisions that often lead to mistakes. Thankfully, we have Sarah to help us with this.

- LN

Control the Chaos with Design Processes and Systems
By Sarah Daniele

I wasn't always the CEO and cofounder of Mydoma Studio. Once upon a not-too-distant past, I was an interior design professional, just like you. Day to day in my design career, I found that I was spending way too much time on administrative tasks. I felt like I was always chasing clients to make design decisions, paying invoices, attending unnecessary meetings, and answering never-ending emails. I needed a way to streamline my processes and make recurring revenue.

As interior designers, we are creatives at heart (left brain), but also analytical (right brain). I knew I wanted to spend more time on the creative aspects of my business. I channeled my frustration and put my right brain to use. I developed my own system that allowed me to reduce redundant administrative work, repeat my design process, and make recurring revenue. Initially, the system was developed for myself to grow my personal design business. It was feedback from designers like you that ultimately initiated the pivot of Mydoma Studio. Fast forward a few years and Mydoma Studio was born: a project- and client-management software built for designers, by designers.

A design business has many moving parts. Having a systematic process will enable you to control the chaos and thrive. I have learned a wealth of knowledge these past ten years. Sit back and grab a cup of coffee, if you don't already have one. Prepare yourself for an eye-opening chapter of truth bombs and analogies. At the end, you'll have the tools and confidence needed to build a design process that works for your business.

Time Management

Are you familiar with the saying "Don't leave money on the table"? In business, you need to make choices that positively impact your revenue because your goal is to run a profitable venture. Your time is money; therefore, how you spend your time affects your bottom line.

Take a moment and think to yourself: in an average week, how often do you feel as though you're putting out fires? Those fires could be ordering products, meeting deadlines, collecting payment, and so on. If more often than not you feel like you're playing catch-up, then you're likely being reactive versus proactive. This is a result of not prioritizing your time.

Prioritizing tasks can very challenging. In order to prioritize, you need to know what's most important to your individual business. The simplest way to break this down is by using the Covey Time Management Grid.

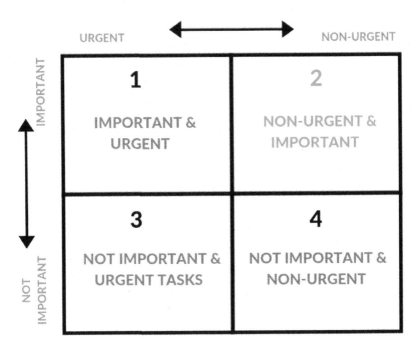

FIG. 1 ADAPTATION OF THE COVEY TIME MANAGEMENT GRID

The Covey Time Management concept is quite simple, but extremely powerful. The x-axis represents urgent activities, and the y-axis represents important activities. We often spend a disproportionate amount of time in Quadrant 1, the "important and urgent" tasks. In today's technology-driven world, everything appears to be urgent when, in fact, it's not. This phenomenon is the result of having instant access at our fingertips through our mobile devices. Think to yourself, is this task really important? What is the impact to my business if I don't get it done "right now"? If you answered yes and the result will be negative, then ask: Is this task truly an unexpected urgent matter that needs my attention, or could I have better planned my time in the first place?

The second commonly-used quadrant is the third: urgent and non-important tasks. This quadrant is a productivity killer because you're working but on the incorrect tasks and activities. Everyday examples of this would be obsessively checking social media platforms and zero-inboxing your email. It is unnecessary to check emails twenty times a day and obsessively refresh your social feeds. Granted, these activities are required, but how and when you go about doing them is essential to maintaining productivity.

In order to be the most effective, you want to spend more time in Quadrant 2, working on important, non-urgent tasks. Yes, you read that correctly. You want to spend most of your time on important, non-urgent tasks. Why would you want to do that? The answer is simple and powerful. These activities are focused around planning and long-term goals. Focusing time on Quadrant 2 ensures you're being proactive with your time. Example tasks include setting up your vendor accounts, implementing project management software, automating social posting, or researching building code requirements for an upcoming project. By spending more time in Quadrant 2, you will have fewer "fires to put out" and your never-ending, urgent to-do list will decrease.

I'm a big believer in taking action. It's one thing to read, so let's go one step further and put it into action. Your homework: for one week, keep track of your daily activities. Use one grid per day and write down all the tasks you complete in the corresponding quadrants. At the end of the week, total up the time spent in each grid to see where you spent the majority of your time. Are you spending at least twenty percent of your time in Quadrant 2? If not, you should be! Keep these words of wisdom in your back pocket: always do what's important first!

You've taken the first major step in controlling the chaos. You now know what tasks you should be working on, but are you being efficient with your time? Are you utilizing tools to track your time for projects and tasks? Time tracking is a necessary evil of running an interior design business. Measuring your time has two benefits back to your business. The first is to ensure you're billing for the time you've actually worked. The second is to provide evidence of how long you spend on particular tasks. If you're not currently tracking your time, you need to make this change. Think of time tracking as your accountability partner.

Are you familiar with the Pomodoro technique? Created by Francesco Cirillo and aptly named after the Pomodoro kitchen timer, this time management technique has you break down tasks into twenty-five-minute increments with small breaks in between. This technique is especially useful for desk work such as sourcing product, design development, blog writing, and so on. These tasks are important to our business, but, without boundaries, they can eat up too much time. Twenty-five minutes may not seem like a long time, but you'd be surprised how much you can get done when you truly focus and time block. As a bonus, this technique encourages breaks. When the timer goes off, take a few minutes to get up and stretch (it's great for the mind and body). If you're not being efficient with your time, you're arguably wasting your most valuable asset and leaving money on the table. Being effective is doing the right things, while being efficient is doing things right.

Be Your Own Champion: Create a process and stick to it

Do you have a system or design process in place to manage your projects from the initial client contact through project closeout? If you answered yes, you're halfway there. If you answered no, you need to establish one. Processes and systems are the backbone of a successful, organized, and profitable business.

Why, you might ask? It's pretty simple. Effective processes and systems allow us to know the answers to the questions before they come up. What forms of payment do you accept? Do you give hard copies of your designs to clients? When and how are contracts signed? How much do you take for a deposit? How and where is that deposit recorded? Where do site pictures and measurements get stored? You get the point. If you're reinventing the wheel for each design project, you're not being effective or efficient with your time.

Take a moment to close your eyes and visualize your design process. How long would it take you to explain your process to a new employee?

Do you have your design process written down or is it stored in your brain? Could you give them a decent overview in under two hours? Does your process feel systematic, A - B - C - D, or would you describe it as a bit chaotic?

No matter the size of your current company, you need to have your design process written down. You need to operate as if your business is one size larger. Control the chaos by being one step ahead versus two steps behind.

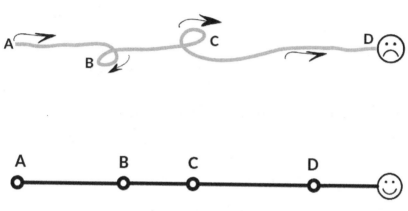

FIG. 2 CHAOTIC PROCESS vs. ORGANIZED PROCESS

I have this incredible chocolate chip recipe. I can't take credit for it because I "borrowed" it from my mother's recipe box many years ago. Here's the thing about this recipe. I have made it an untold amount of times, and each time I follow that recipe exactly. I don't diverge because I know if I follow it, I will get perfectly golden-brown bottoms with a little crunch on the outside and be irresistibly chewy. Think of your design process as a "recipe" and your "ingredients" as your tools and knowledge. As interior design professionals, we all have the same ingredients, but how and in what order we use those ingredients determines the final outcome of our recipe, or, in this example, our design project.

Take a moment to think about your own "design process recipe." Do you follow the same order of operations each time? Or do you mix it up from time to time? A process is absolutely necessary, but you also must be able to repeat your process. If you can't repeat it, you cannot grow your business. Every business is different. There is no one-size-fits-all when it comes to the design process. If you have an existing process, write it down. If you do not have a concise process, it's time to develop one. To help you get started, I have included a list of key activities and milestones to review. Consider using a mind map tool to build out your process. It's a visual representation of the order of activities and milestones that must be completed along the project path. The end goal is to understand how the activities are connected and what needs to be completed before the next phase can begin. For example, you shouldn't measure the project before a deposit is taken and a contract is signed.

Here are some major activities/ milestones to consider in your own design process:

Initial client consultation
Client/project intake questionnaire
Contract development, signing, and taking deposits
Site measuring and photographs
Design development
Product sourcing
Design presentation
Drawing/design sign off
Client meetings
Product ordering/Delivery timelines
Installation/build phase
Deficiencies review and resolution
Collecting payment
Project closeout and after sales

Work Smart, Not Hard: A repeatable process is the secret sauce to growing an interior design business

It's one thing to know what you should be doing, but how you should be doing it is a whole other challenge. Let's dive a bit deeper into efficiency and talk some more about cookies. In this scenario, you need to bake not one, but five, batches of chocolate chip cookies. Do you go to the fridge five separate times for the eggs or do you go once? Maximizing your time is obviously of the utmost importance. The order in which you complete activities is equally as important as how you complete the activities. Instead of going to the fridge five times for eggs, or, in this example, writing five emails explaining your services, rates, and process, why not provide a new client welcome package in advance of their project starting?

Let's break this down. Creating the welcome package in advance is time-consuming. You'll need to create a template, brand it to your company, and fill out the information. Spending the time now is being proactive with your time. The use of the welcome package is going to answer clients' questions and concerns before they arise later on in the project. Go one step further and include a high-level breakdown of your design process. You'll exceed their expectations and they'll trust you through the entire process. A client welcome package is a tool that you can use repeatedly, and this will maximize your time.

I have a favor to ask. Please stop wasting time in Quadrant 3 by reinventing the wheel each time. Develop a design process and use technology to your advantage. Create templates for contracts, questionnaires, welcome packages, measure guides, and so on. Prevent fires from ever forming by being both effective and efficient with your time. A repeatable design process keeps the project on track and on budget, exceeds the clients' expectations, and will lead to referrals for future projects.

Now that you have your design process, let's go one step further and make note of when something is or isn't working. Don't be afraid to iterate. From time to time, internal and external events will force you to review your process and make changes as necessary. Internal events are changes in your business. For example, you've added team members, or you've decided to outsource your 3D renderings. An external factor is a change outside of your business. These changes are out of your control but can affect how your business is managed. An example of an external event is the increase and adoption of technology. Clients are educated, wanting to share in the design process, and also want to work and pay online. This major change in client behavior will and should nudge you to review your process to adapt.

There are consequences if you aren't willing to adapt your process. If you have a process that's always worked, that's no excuse not to improve. You're always personally self-improving, so why not improve your business? Just because something is working, or it's the way you've always done it, doesn't mean it's the best way. By staying the same, you could be leaving projects, clients, and opportunities on the table. If your process is broken, fix it. If it's working, be aware of internal and external factors that may require you to make changes!

You Don't Need to Wear ALL the Hats All the Time

Running and growing an interior design business is not for the faint of heart. It's a marathon, not a sprint. Unlike most marathons, this one requires you to wear a lot of hats. It's unrealistic to assume if you're not good at something in your business, you simply won't do it. Sometimes you'll have to do activities or act in roles that don't play to your strengths. There is incredible power in knowing where you need help. These tasks could be future hires or tasks that you outsource.

Think of the four quadrants we discussed earlier. Let's say improving your SEO is a priority for the business. You could invest the time in learning everything there is to know about SEO and make the changes to your website yourself. This would be incredibly time-consuming. Or you could do a baseline level of research and understand the problem you're looking to solve. Then outsource to a company or individual you trust to make the changes for you. Educating yourself with a base knowledge is incredibly useful for navigating conversations in areas you're not an expert in. It will also give you the confidence to know you've picked a reputable business to work with.

Outsourcing is incredibly empowering and will enable you to be more efficient with your time. A tale of caution, though. Be careful about what and how much you outsource, especially in the beginning stages. If you outsource too much, it can be quite costly and you can lose control of the process. Outsourcing should save you time and enable you to control the chaos, not add more.

Here is another scenario. Let's say you have an established business. In the past, you've always done your 3D renderings either by hand or in-house. With an increasing client base, you'd like to outsource the renderings to speed up the process and free up your time. Try working with the outsourcing company or individual on a smaller project. Get the kinks worked out before over-committing. Outsourcing is incredibly useful, but be cautious that you don't sacrifice quality for time. Whether you're outsourcing graphic design, website design, social media, SEO, or drafting services, ensure you have a clear understanding of what you're expecting to get.

You can't do everything, nor should you. If you try to do everything, your quality of work may suffer. Worst of all, you might burn out and build resentment towards your business. Play to your strengths, not your weaknesses. Outsource when needed, but make sure you're always being effective and efficient.

Conclusion

I hope this chapter has given you insight into the importance of creating a repeatable design process and understanding the difference between efficiency and effectiveness. I hope that you've found answers to your problems and feel inspired to either create or improve your existing design process.

Lesson #1, Time management
Stop wasting your time on urgent, unimportant tasks. Do the important tasks to your business. Be effective with your time.

Lesson #2, Create a repeatable process
Use the right tools for the job to maximize your efficiency.

Lesson #3, Play to your strengths, not your weaknesses
Stop trying to be the "Pinterest Mom of perfection" in regard to your business. You can't be an expert at everything.

Running and growing an interior design business doesn't need to be chaotic. By using the right tools to manage your processes and systems, you will lay a stable foundation to grow your business. You and your team will continue to thrive. Your clients will be happier and trust you. If you have questions, reach out to your design community of peers. The Mydoma Studio Designers Community is an excellent resource to tap into. Ask questions and learn from one another. Whether you're a solopreneur or established team, remember that building a successful interior design business begins and ends with your design process.

References

Jackson, E. (2012, July 24). "The Only Thing You Need to Remember about The Seven Habits of Highly Effective People." *Forbes*. Retrieved from https://www.forbes.com/sites/ericjackson/2012/07/24/the-only-thing-you-need-to-remember-about-the-seven-habits-of-highly-effective-people/#4bf8ae3d67f7

Sutevski, D. (2018). "Efficiency and Effectiveness Matrix." Retrieved from https://www.entrepreneurshipinabox.com/394/efficiency-effectiveness-matrix/

US Geological Survey Department of Employee and Organizational Development. (2011). "Time Management Grid." Retrieved from https://www2.usgs.gov/humancapital/documents/TimeManagementGrid.pdf

If you are either a regular listener of my podcast, or if you have read my first book, The Making of A Well-Designed Business®, then you know exactly how I feel about systems and the tremendous value they provide in creating a successful business. That also means you know that working within systems was not in my nature and I have no innate super powers in this area. That's right, zippo.

I understand how hard it can be, how daunting and how time-consuming it is to create systems. I have said a dozen times how lucky I have been to learn from my husband Vin the undeniable importance of having stated, repeatable processes and systems. I have, with time and experience, learned how often a system has saved us from a costly mistake, how many times it has helped my installer "think like LuAnn" because LuAnn "does it this way." Because of our systems, we have been able to train new employees faster and more efficiently, sell more product, create more referrals, and create more revenue in our business.

I have also learned that not being good at systems and not liking systems is not a justifiable reason to avoid having systems. If you are in business, you must address it, and if you truly struggle with it, platforms like Mydoma Studio can be a game changer for you. But make no mistake about it, even Mydoma Studio is not the entire answer. You can buy software and sign up for all the productivity apps you can get your hands on, but if you don't then create a system for utilizing the platform or the app, it is useless. The platform must become part of your system, or one step in your process. If it doesn't, that would be like buying running shoes and thinking you're going to run a marathon just because you have them in your closet. You have to put the work into everything you do. There's just no way around it.

At Window Works, our systems have systems and our systems are the oil that keeps our machine running smoothly and efficiently every day, week, and year.

To Sarah's point, we actually schedule time to intentionally work in quadrant 2 (checking on orders, following up with clients, scheduling social media posts), so we experience way less time on frantic phone calls from clients, missing information or product on install day, and all of the chaos that exists in Quadrant 1.

Running a business always has its ups and downs—that comes with the territory—but defined systems are the key to taming the crazy and to ensure you are doing your very best each day.

- LN

About the Author

Sarah Daniele is the CEO and cofounder of Mydoma Studio. She is an industry-leading design expert with ten years of design experience. Sarah understands how important it is to have systems and processes in place to effectively manage and grow your interior design business. Sarah and Mydoma Studio have been featured on the popular *A Well-Designed Business®* Podcast, in *Home Accents Today, Editor at Large,* and *Kitchen & Bath Design News.*

Sarah has appeared on LuAnn's podcast twice, on episodes 91 and 177:

https://luannnigara.com/91-sarah-daniele-co-founder-ceo-of-mydoma-studio/

https://luannnigara.com/177-power-talk-friday-sarah-daniele-ceo-of-mydoma-studio-is-back-to-tell-us-what-s-new-for-you-at-mydoma-studio/

CHAPTER 6

Claire Jefford

C laire is one of the two authors among us who is actually a practicing
interior designer. Her perspective and her insights come from the
direct experience of doing what you do. Of course, as evidenced
by this book and so many other business books, you don't have to do the
same work as someone to teach them sound advice. (Are Gary V., Barbara
Corcoran, or Gary McKeown interior designers?)

Still, when you read Claire's chapter, remember that she stands in your
shoes every day, going on consults, talking about budgets and timelines,
and managing clients' expectations. While her exact business model may
not mirror yours, clients are clients and expectations are expectations, no
matter the type of design firm you have.

You've heard me say it countless times on the podcast: when agreements
are made before the project begins, it not only provides clarity for all, but it
also significantly reduces conflicts during the project.

Between her coaching, the business packages she has created, her
YouTube channel and her IG Live videos, Claire is always teaching and
inspiring us to pay attention to the nuances of the client relationship. In
this chapter, Claire shares what she has identified as the most important
areas to address in order to set yourself, your client, and the project up
for success. While there are no guarantees she was wearing pants during
the writing of this chapter, I can guarantee Claire delivers it in her typical
entertaining and straightforward approach.

- LN

Managing Client Expectations
By Claire Jefford

What would it mean to your business to have clients who always pay on time, never question your billing, and value all the hard work that you do? It is possible.

I'll tell you a story about the spring of 2011, when I got my first paying client. This client was neither a friend, nor a friend of a friend, nor a neighbor—which are all fine to have as clients, by the way. This was the first client who hired my services whom I had no personal connection to. As a mature student on the verge of attaining my certification for interior decorating, booking this client felt as though Christmas had come early!

She found me through a local home show, where as a student of the interior decorating program, I had featured some of my mood boards and included business cards at a booth representing the college program. I was excited about this opportunity, although I wasn't really expecting anything to come from it. Merely greeting people as they visited the booth and answering questions about decorating was thrilling enough for me on its own.

The following week, I received a phone call. On the other end was a woman who said she loved the color palette from one of the boards that I had created. She agreed to my consultation fee of seventy-five dollars for a two-hour meeting, and we booked the appointment. (Note: seven years later, my two-hour consultation fee is six hundred dollars). Early on in my business, I also used to do a free half-hour meet-and-greet, which was a great way to get my foot in the door and in front of potential new clients. Learn more about how this worked for me in this video "To Charge or Not To Charge" and see also my video "The Initial Consultation: What to Charge."

Fast forward to a few weeks into helping my new clients with their decorating needs, the following realizations were quickly sinking in:

1) I had totally underestimated the time it would take to complete the initial requested outline scope of work. (This does happen and is expected as part of the learning curve when you are new.)

2) My clients were emailing me a lot, often questioning my recommendations, with total disregard as to whether it was the weekend or late at night.

3) Despite the fact that I had charged a flat fee, scope creep was starting to happen. Meetings that were initially intended to focus on ideas for updating their living and dining room were snowballing into requests for sourcing and layout ideas for tile in their main entry and kitchen, in addition to questions about whether they should redo their main stairs and, if so, in what stain. I would also wake up to find emails in my inbox asking, "Would you mind also quickly giving us some recommendations of what type of a runner we should consider for the stairs?" or "We'd love a few suggestions for window treatment styles for the kids' bedrooms," and "If we paint the kitchen cabinetry to update that area, what paint color do you think would work best?"

4) They wanted to know where I had sourced some of the items, asking for details so they could take a look either online or go to the store on their own time.

5) I received delayed responses to emails or didn't receive confirmation of future appointments I had tentatively booked with them. Despite the project starting off full steam ahead with the clients very enthusiastic about it all, as time went on, a few weeks would go by where I was waiting for them to find out whether they wished to move forward with selections and purchases.

6) No way was I getting any decent photos from this project. Many of my recommendations were not being implemented and some of their choices did not complement other elements or lead to a finished look.

I think you get the point and see the pattern happening here, right? If you've been in the business for any length of time already, I'm sure you are nodding your head right along with me!

How did this go from being my "dream client project" to a complete nightmare that I wasn't sure how to wake up from?

Let's take a look at how this type of client and similar scenarios can make you feel:

- Undervalued
- Resentful
- Frustrated
- As if you've been taken advantage of
- Like a failure
- As though you are working for free

These are dangerous feelings to have because they can often lead to:

- Burnout
- Low self-esteem and a lack of confidence in your abilities
- Running a business that is not profitable
- Giving up as an entrepreneur

The good news is, there is a much better way and there are really great clients out there waiting for you!

In fact, the best clients, your IDEAL clients, are going to be the clients who respect that you take control from the offset of your working relationship together when you outline your processes and establish boundaries, they appreciate the incredible value you bring to a project, and they are willing to have open and honest discussions about money and a realistic investment amount needed for their project.

Before we address how to get those ideal clients, first we need to look at why this happens. It can be easy to presume that most people know what you do as an interior design professional, but the truth is that many home owners:

- Don't understand the extent of the value you bring to a project.
- Don't know what goes on behind the scenes in this business or how you work.
- Have a lack of trust and respect for what you do, because they don't know the finer details of how you help. After all, your job is fun, right?!
- May not put the same monetary value into your service as what they do for a product or something that is tangible.

People have this mindset because:

- Shows like the ones on HGTV can make our roles as design professionals appear carefree and exciting.
- You avoided important conversations about realistic timelines and actual estimated costs for the project.
- You are unsure of how to take control of the working relationship.
- Organized processes are missing from your business model.
- Building your portfolio is more of a priority than watching out for possible red flags.
- You are not charging enough for your consultation fee and services.

How can you stop these situations from arising and eliminate these types of feelings? By following the mantra that I use for my business every day:

- Manage clients' expectations
- Educate your client
- Communicate effectively

(NOTE: This mantra should not be limited to client relationships only. You need to extend these principles to your trades, suppliers, and those whom you network with in order to have a completely well-rounded and effective business model. For the purpose of my chapter in this book, we will stick to focusing on clients.)

When, Where, and How Do We Start Managing Client Expectations?

Begin by establishing your brand's values and effectively communicating your story to your audience.

1. Website and Branding

What type of client is your website targeting?

In today's world where everyone turns to the internet as a resource for all things, your potential clients will probably find you either through your website or through your social-media posts. Even if the client comes to you through a referral, the first step anyone will probably take after being passed your information is to head to the almighty Google. They want to find out more about you and what you have to offer.

Here are eight tips for great web design that will help you attract your ideal clients:

> ➤ A clean look with easy navigation that includes a simple menu to follow at the top of every page.
>
> ➤ Your home page should make it abundantly clear what it is that you do and include a photo of you.
>
> ➤ Your footer needs to include the specific locations you service.
>
> ➤ Your portfolio must consist of PROFESSIONAL PHOTOS ONLY. Don't compromise on this. Quality photos = quality clients. Even when you think the photos you took yourself on your phone are pretty good, they are seldom as good as or near the quality of a professional photographer.
>
> ➤ Do not include "before" photos in your portfolio; save these for a separate page or for blog posts. You do not want a potential client mistaking one of your "before" images for an "after" photo.
>
> ➤ The about page needs to have a professional headshot of you. I'll give you bonus points if you add an introductory video! (See link

to video 1 at the end of the chapter.) Your message in the copy here needs to be all about *how you can help your ideal client*. Hit on their pain points and share how you can solve their problems and ease their feelings of overwhelm and confusion. Don't list your favorite type of pasta or what you think is the best movie of all time. The new follower to your page doesn't care about you yet; they only care about *how you can help them*.

➤ Your services page should clearly outline your services, including any packages you offer. Bullet point each offering and include your "starting from" rates. Adding visuals of what you provide in your packages makes it easier for potential clients to understand what you do and how you can help; i.e. images of a mood board, rendering, and/or sketch.

➤ The contact page needs to be easy to find and any requested information should be straightforward for people to enter. Be sure to ask for a name, email address, phone number, their location, and a box where they can add a message about their project. I'll give you more bonus points if you ask about their budget and if you include a box they can tick that asks them to subscribe to your email list! Following the completion of the contact form, they should receive a notification that confirms their message has been delivered and includes copy with an estimated time of when they can expect a follow-up from your office.

2. Blog Posts and Social Media

These forums provide the perfect opportunity to strut your stuff! It's now easier than ever to hop on social-media sites to immediately connect with your audience. I especially love the IGTV channel to share weekly tips, and I use this not only for decorating tips, but also to share videos of my business processes. (See link 2 at the end of the chapter.)

Why not go live from your Facebook page while on the site of a current project or photoshoot? People love seeing sneak peaks and getting a "behind the scenes" glimpse into the world of interior design.

Posts that poll your audience or ask for their opinions are also widely popular. It's true that not everyone who follows you or subscribes to your blog will hire your services, but remember that even if you get comments, likes, or shares, this type of engagement is vital to the success of your online branding strategies. Your social media and blog posts keep you top of mind with your audience. Your posts should be about relevant content pertaining to what you do and how you can help solve a problem. Show people why you are someone to follow!

Here's where many people go wrong with their social media posts. In terms of content, I appreciate that sharing your new favourite wallpaper or the latest trends you saw at Highpoint Market can be fun to write about. Peppering your blogs with this type of content on occasion is totally acceptable, as these posts show followers that you have your finger on the pulse of what's happening in the industry. However, you ideally want to create content that is addressing (and solving!) your potential clients' biggest struggles. Consider what your most Frequently Asked Questions (FAQs) are when you have someone inquiring about your services on a phone call or during the initial consultation.

Also, what are the biggest hurdles that you encounter when you are working with a client? Remember in the first part of this chapter when I detailed my headaches with my first real client? Go back to where I listed why burnout and resentment occur and draw your inspiration for content creation from there.

Videos

The fastest way to connect with your audience and one of the most effective ways to communicate your message online is via video. I've created videos that outline my processes for working with clients. These videos not only outline the features of what I do, but I also clearly explain the benefits of what a potential client can expect when working with me on a project. (See video link 2 at the end of the chapter.)

In an effort to reduce the "sticker shock" that can come with quoting estimates for custom projects, I recorded a couple of videos where I disclose all costs of some fully custom rooms we've designed. These videos enable me to educate potential clients on typical budgets for our custom decorating services. Once people understand realistic costs and have signed our Letter of Agreement and are on retainer with us, there are no surprises or dropped jaws when I quote estimates of pricing for a finished space.

If you don't like video, I get it. (I'm disappointed and think you need to just hit the record button … but I get it.) Write blog posts that are of similar topics. You can link to these posts time and time again, sending them to potential clients to show them the value behind what it is that you do.

To gain confidence and learn about the who, what, where, why, when and how of video, check out my Video for Profits course (link 3 at the end of the chapter).

NOTE: For social media, you will initially need to test which platforms work best for attracting your ideal client. Over time, as social media continues to evolve and algorithms change, you may need to alter your social media calendar and online marketing strategies.

In order to be truly effective in your social media efforts, you must be consistent with your postings. This is by far one of the biggest challenges as a business owner. To make it easier and to plan for success, set up a social media calendar and schedule regular weekly posts on your top three social media platforms.

Write a new blog post at least once a month. This will help with your website's Search Engine Optimization (SEO). Your main priority is to get your audience onto your website and signed up to your email list. Other social media platforms are unpredictable with pivoting algorithms and ever-changing rules. Your website and email list are the only tools that you control in the online world.

3. Share Past Experiences with Clients

As you take on more clients, you will learn from every project, giving you more confidence with each new job. When you can draw from past experiences, you provide proof of your authority. Being able to explain why something worked and why things may have gone wrong is very powerful. Use those as examples to reinforce the value that you provide and how you will handle similar circumstances should they arise on another project.

Discuss these situations in person at the consultation meeting and write about them in both your blog and in your social media posts. Speaking from experience gives your viewers more confidence in you and in your ability to successfully manage a variety of challenges with creative solutions.

4. Streamline Your Processes

This could be an entire chapter all on its own!

Since my background is in human resources, I can tell you that having organized processes in your business is everything. From the very first phone call to the final reveal of a project, having your processes nailed down is essential for running a successful firm and managing clients' expectations. When clients see that you have exceptional organizational skills and specific steps that you diligently follow for each phase of a project, they will have much more confidence in you.

Taking the time up front to carefully outline every step of the process to your client minimizes potential disappointments and misunderstandings as you move forward through the execution stages of the project.

For example, we recently finished working on a second project with a fabulous client. Initially, they intended to do a few different projects all at one time. We asked what their budget was and sat down to review a cost schedule of furnishings with them. This exercise entails entering details into a spreadsheet of each item required to finish the space and we include an estimated range of pricing for each piece. For example: Dining room chair x 8 estimated at $650 - $850 each = $5,200 - $6,800.

As we began working our way through the spreadsheet together, it didn't take long for the client to see that their initial idea of an investment amount was not a sufficient number to complete everything on their wish list. Therefore, we suggested doing the scope of work in phases and they agreed.

This is a great exercise that provides an excellent opportunity for you to talk about money and educate your client, which in turn equates to managing their expectations.

5. Discuss Money and Possible Setbacks up Front

As you saw in the previous example, speaking with your clients about estimated costs for a project is a crucial step that can never be overlooked. This same mindset needs to be applied when stating your own fees and requesting payment. I'll go into more detail on this a little further into the chapter.

Just as it's important to discuss money, you always need to be up front about what could potentially go wrong on a project. When things don't go according to plan, it doesn't mean that you weren't able to competently do your job. It simply means that you cannot control the outcome of every situation. This is especially true when it comes to ordering product. For example, back orders of items will happen from time to time. Shipments may get delayed not only at border crossings or when leaving the manufacturer's warehouse but may also get damaged in transit.

When orders get delayed, your tradespeople may have to move on to another job while waiting for the product to arrive. Then when the materials or items are ready, the trades may not yet be finished from the job they moved on to while waiting for the back-ordered product and some further delays have resulted.

Obviously, while you don't want to scare the crap out of your client and send them running for the hills in fear, you do need to let them know that these types of delays are possible in order to carefully manage their expectations.

The key here is that you want the focus to be about not what will go wrong, but how you will confidently deal with these situations should they arise. Your role is to give your clients complete assurance that you will be there to take care of everything as quickly and as smoothly as possible. That's why they are paying you the big bucks!

6. Be You

Through experience and over time, you will be sculpting your brand, gaining confidence, and building stronger relationships with those in the industry. Eventually, all of this will become very natural to you and you will gain an understanding of who you are and what you stand for. Don't compare yourself to others. I know that this is hard not to do, especially with all the noise in our online worlds.

Instead of measuring yourself against anyone else, take inspiration when you need to from someone you admire, but don't get caught up in trying to be something you are not. Stay in your own lane and be the best version of you that you can be.

Setting the Tone

Have you ever noticed that the way that someone approaches you or speaks to you can incite a reaction of similar tone and attitude? For example, when my husband has a lousy customer-service experience, he's ready to go in with all guns blazing! I say to him, "What's that going to do? How do you expect the person on the other end of your aggression to respond?" We all know how that one goes. The person on the receiving end is going to instantly get their back up.

However, when you approach mishaps in a way where you can calmly convey your disappointment and feelings of frustration, the person on the receiving end is likely to be more empathetic and willing to help find a solution to your problem.

Discovery call (first half): Your potential client has seen your posts on social media and checked out your website. They are excited at the possibility of working with you on their project. It's time for the discovery call.

Even if you have someone else answer your phone, you'll want to make sure that they adhere to the following list. Here you want to set the tone for the way that you work. Remember that you are vetting this potential client, just as much as they are vetting you as their potential designer. Let's treat this like a soccer game where it's a game of two halves. Make no mistake: you should always take the lead offense role and dominate the game, in a nonaggressive way.

If you have the completed information that they sent via your contact page on your website and this is the next touch point, be sure to have those details to hand, so you can refer to them during the conversation.

The Who, Where, When, and What:

- Verify that you have their correct name and contact details.
- Find out where they are located and how they heard about you.
- When do they need you?
- What are details of their project?

I ask these questions in this order because first, you want to be able to refer to them by their name. It's important to ensure that you have their contact details in case you get disconnected or need to call them back.

Depending on the areas you serve, finding out where they are located is especially important. Before they go into detail about their project or before you offer any pricing, be sure you know where they are located. This could determine whether you will take on a project and if you need to add extra costs for travel fees before providing quotes.

Finding out where they heard about you and tracking this information for your own reference will assist you in knowing where to put your efforts into future marketing strategies.

Asking about the timelines is important because this could reveal a lot about the type of client they will be. If they have left things to the last minute and need you in the next few days, this can be a huge red flag. When potential clients tell me that they've waited years to renovate and they are doing their due diligence in these early planning stage, that is music to my ears.

Last, finding out details of the project will enable you to decide if this is the type of project you wish to take on and whether you offer services relevant to their needs.

Discovery call (second half): The way in which you handle yourself on the call overall will largely determine in the client's mind whether or not you are the best fit for their project. But it's also during this second half of the conversation that you get the opportunity to really shine. Now that the formalities are out of the way and you have an understanding about their struggles and needs, you can effectively communicate how you can help.

- Advise them of the services you offer. State both the features of what you do and the benefits as well. For example, you may tell them, "We offer 3D design packages that allow you to see your space before you start your project."
- Confidently list your consultation fees and starting price points for your services.
- Clearly outline the process for booking an appointment and include when payment is required, as well as your accepted methods of payment. Be sure also to include any additional fees for travel.
- When you end the call, make it crystal clear what the next steps will be, so they know what to expect after you hang up the phone.

After the phone call, I always like to send an email with links to my website and services page. To add further value and based on the details of our conversation, I also include links to videos or blog posts pertaining to their project or design dilemma. I send them possible dates for the consultation meeting and instructions on my booking/payment process.

Initial consultation: Your processes leading up to the consultation are there to build trust with your client and are the foundation for a solid, mutually respectful working relationship for the future. Now that you are face to face, depending on your business model, here are my suggestions for the consultation meeting to continue with this blissfully happy relationship between you and your new client:

The following are essential in managing expectations:

- Review your Welcome Letter or an Outline of Services with your client.
- Show clients examples of past projects and work that you've done, such as presentation packages with CAD drawings, renderings, mood boards, or price lists so they know EXACTLY what to expect from your services.
- Have a list of Frequently Asked Questions for your client.
- Have a binder of any documentation you may need at the consultation meeting.
- Depending on your business model, be prepared with a Letter of Agreement and to advise on how you will collect your retainer in order to move forward with further services.

Important Note about the LOA/Contract

Leaving a client with the Letter of Agreement (LOA) or sending it after the meeting and not reviewing it with them is a huge mistake. Reviewing the LOA with your client should be seen as a fabulous opportunity to open up further discussions on how you work and why you work the way you do. This is the perfect time to provide your client with assurance and peace of mind, so they know that they are partnering with a straight shooter who talks openly about money, handling trades, the purchasing process, your hours of availability, and how best to communicate with one another throughout the course of the project.

Effectively communicating the ways in which you work, by using various tools and resources to educate potential clients on how you can help with their project, means you will have thoughtfully managed their expectations. To learn more about my processes, obtain all my drafted emails and more than fifteen templates, including my step-by-step process flow chart with video walk through, and video footage of me on the discovery call and in an initial consultation meeting, check out my comprehensive three-in-one bundle that also includes a business starter pack and LOA with video. See attachment 1.4 below.

Final Thoughts

Sadly, many in our industry underestimate the value that they bring to a design or decorating project. Because this comes easily to us and because what we offer is often advice compared to something tangible, many design professionals give services and time away for free.

Keep in mind that you are a key player in influencing major changes and decisions in a family's biggest investment! Good clients are out there. They will trust you with that fun yet enormous responsibility of designing their home, choosing finishes, and getting the finer details of the custom furniture orders just right. We take on a ton of liability in this business and are always learning something new with every client and every project. To pivot and adapt to this constantly changing landscape, we work hard and have a passion for what we do like no other industry. Never underestimate the value in that.

Take control, get organized, gain confidence, manage expectations, minimize stress in your business, get better clients, and charge what you are worth!

Resources

1. Introductory video on my website: clairejefford.com/interior-design/#services

2. IGTV Episode #11: instagram.com/tv/BmbSImwgaUu/?utm_source=ig_share_sheet&igshid=6ehy3rg7qykg

3. Video for Profits clairejefford.com/product/video-for-profits/

4. 3-in-1 Package clairejefford.com/product/three-in-one-package/

5. My YouTube Channel
   youtube.com/channel/UCQk_aV9ZOlCfr-Ia9FFvs5g

As you began to read Claire's chapter, you may have thought to yourself, "Why is she talking about my website and my social media strategies? I thought we were going to learn about managing client expectations."

Managing client expectations begins with the very first impressions of you and your company. More often than not, this is through your online presence. After learning about you, when a client ultimately speaks with you, if you have portrayed yourself and your work accurately, it begins to instill trust. This small but important touch point is so valuable in your relationship with them. We often say earning a new client is like dating someone. Think about it: what if you found a profile on a dating site and liked everything you learned, only to meet on the first date and find that the impression and the reality are not aligned? Even if the reality is something you could like, you have already started on the wrong foot.

Be you, be you, be you, everywhere.

Your website and social media presence are where you start to teach your client how you will work with them and how they can work with you. Your website can explain the overview of your process and the types of projects you handle, allowing prospective clients to imagine themselves working with you.

Claire's message emphasizes that successful projects start with agreements and communication from the outset. It begins with your website, continues with the intake call, the consultation, the LOA, and lasts throughout entire project to completion.

One way to figure out what your process is to ask yourself, "What will I do and what won't I do?"

- Will I take text messages?
- Will I bill monthly or weekly?
- Will I do one revision or two revisions?
- Will I only deliver a "reveal" install?
- Will I do consultations on weekends?
- Will I work with a client's trades?
- Will I provide 3-D drawings?
- Will I source only to the trade?
- Will I charge for consultations?
- Will I share discounts?

There are no right or wrong answers to these questions. There is no "one way"; there is only "your way." One of you may be a side hustler and therefore prefers to see clients on weekends, while another may have a family, so weekends are a no-work zone. It is up to you how you will work. The mistake is not being clear about "your way" until there is a problem. If a client brings in their trade, you want to yell and cry foul, but did you explain that was not an option before starting the project? Or did you assume "they should know that"?

Recall a negative interaction with a client. It could have been last week or years ago. No matter how mad you were, no matter how clear it was to you the client was in the wrong, I challenge you now to come up with at least one thing, no matter how small, you could have done to avoid the conflict.

I promise you, in every single problem on a project, a moment happened where you did not manage expectations fully. You either avoided a conversation, avoided a decision, or avoided an action, and that, my friend, is precisely where you could have avoided the problem.

Know your process, explain it in clear language, and, as Claire advises, present your LOA in person, going over all the details. Conduct yourself as *the professional you are. If things go off the rails, as they sometimes will, you can calmly refer to the agreements you both made and work toward getting back on the same track.*

- *LN*

About the Author

Claire Jefford began her award-winning interior decorating firm in 2011 and is now also an interior design business coach. Claire is passionate about having organized processes and marketing strategies, and she loves creating videos. Voted the Number Three Top Influencer in 2018, Claire does live video broadcasts from various events across North America. She also has a highly active Facebook group, Interior Design Business Strategies, with over three thousand members worldwide.

Claire has appeared on LuAnn's podcast twice, on episodes 237 and 325:

> https://luannnigara.com/237-claire-jefford-how-to-get-more-clients-with-video-content/

> https://luannnigara.com/325-claire-jefford-create-valuable-content-to-sell-through-your-website/

CHAPTER 7

Eileen Hahn

D o you have employees now, or even one employee? Do you have intentions of growing your firm beyond its current size? If the answer is yes to either of these questions, then I promise you that this chapter may be the most important chapter of all of them in propelling your interior design firm to success and profitability.

We both know that you can't grow if your pricing structure isn't profitable, you can't grow if your marketing and your branding aren't on point, and you certainly can't grow if you cannot close the sale. However, right up there with having impeccable systems for every aspect of your business, knowing how to find, interview, hire, train, and develop your team is essential in building the foundation of your business. Without this information and skill set, spending time and money on marketing to attract clients whom you cannot properly serve is counterproductive. Your employees are the very extension of you. They represent your brand, your company, and your values to your clients. If you are not represented with excellence and they do not execute their activities with excellence, all the marketing in the world will not grow your business. The goal is to have your marketing, your messaging, and your systems in place to attract the ideal client, but it is how your client is handled and how the project is executed that will create a client for life and a client who will refer you. For this, you need exceptional employees who are as invested in the well-being of your clients and the success of your firm as you are.

How do you create a team like this? As Eileen explains, one exceptional employee at a time.

You will learn in Eileen's examples, because employees are individual human beings, each with unique strengths, personality traits, and goals, it requires you, as the leader, to identify, develop, nurture, and reward each employee in the style that respects, fulfills, and speaks to them. The most gratifying part is that when you do this, everyone wins: your employee, your client, and your company.

As you read her chapter, take notice of the example of Michael and Kim, which can teach us a little bonus lesson as business owners. Eileen's objective in sharing this example is primarily to teach us the importance of continually coaching our employees to reach their potential. I'd like you to also consider this example when dealing with your own clients. In other words, allow "Michael" to coach you here too. Often when a client does not choose to hire us, it is because we have not heard them, or we have not understood their challenges and their motivations for considering a project. Put yourself in Kim's place. Think about projects you didn't get and ask if you have been guilty of being too focused on what you wanted for the design project rather than truly listening to your clients. Then put yourself in Michael's place, as principal of your firm, the coach responsible for leading your employees to do their best. It is imperative to understand both sides of this lesson.

Now, let's take a look at how to build a team that you will be proud to have represent you and your firm.

- LN

How to staff an interior design firm one exceptional employee at a time

By Eileen Hahn

If you want to grow a business, you need an exceptional staff. Thinking about how to staff a growing business can be daunting. There are too many variables and people. Where do you find them? How do you train them? What to do?

When I teach organizations how to hire and lead people, I never talk about hiring a whole team, even if they need hundreds of people. It is always about how to find, hire, and lead one exceptional person. When you learn how to lead one person really well, that knowledge and skill act as the basis for finding and leading two, three, four, even ten people or more.

In this chapter, you'll learn how to keep first things first. You'll learn how to approach your problem in a way that's manageable. You'll discover how to hire, train, develop, and lead one single extraordinary person well, and how to use that understanding to grow your business to the size it deserves. Whether this is your first employee or you already have a staff of twelve, twenty or more, focus on just one person. It starts with leading one exceptional person well.

What does one exceptional employee look like?
They will:

- Exceed your performance expectations in quality, production volume, and results.
- Come to work with a positive attitude every day and love their job.
- Go above and beyond what is expected and be committed to the success of the organization.
- Ignite cooperation and teamwork.
- Inspire team members to do more, be more, and achieve more.

An exceptional employee brings fire and energy to the business. They raise the bar on quality, customer service, employee experience, culture, and business results. They often suggest new revenue streams. They develop innovative approaches to conducting business. They streamline processes that save the company time and money. They build a positive culture because they believe in your vision. They come to work excited to make your vision happen every day. They make the organization stronger, more effective, more profitable, and more fun.

I have worked with large and small organizations staffed with exceptional employees. To see these employees at work is a joy. The business hums and the financial results are tremendous. People high-five in the halls. You hear laughter in meetings. You come across informal gatherings engaged in creative brainstorming. People work past five because no one has any idea what time it is. People show up to work at ease, being themselves, using natural talents/strengths/superpowers, and perform extraordinarily well. When I talk to an exceptional employee they say, "I love my job. I can't wait to come to work because it feels great to work with exceptional team members to produce extraordinary results that help us realize our vision."

You can create an organization of exceptional employees. I have found that companies that consistently deliver year-over-year high profit margins, and receive exceptional customer and employee experience ratings, also hire and nurture exceptional employees. How do they do that? It starts with one employee at a time. So, how do you find that one exemplar and help them flourish?

Eleven pivotal management principles are integral to finding and nurturing an exceptional employee. Each principle propels performance, results, and morale in a positive direction. Once you implement these principles with one employee, you will have the knowledge and skills to lead an entire staff of exceptional people! It all starts with hiring the right person.

Pivotal Management Principles

1. Hire with specificity

Is an exceptional person born or made? The answer is a little of both. Everyone can excel in a job aligned with their natural talents. When a person does what they do best, there is an opportunity for excellence. We all come equipped with innate skills, talents, and superpowers. We don't have to try or do anything special; they are just our natural gifts. These superpowers come fluidly and easily to us. Superpowers are not just our strengths. They are not just skills that we are very good at. They are strengths that we enjoy exercising. People who use their superpowers at work say, "I can't believe they are paying me to do this. I would do it for free. I never want to retire, because I love what I do." Superpowers are the gifts and talents we want to use on the job. When we use those gifts, we have the opportunity to be extraordinary in what we do.

To hire an exceptional employee, you need to be very specific about what you want them to do and how you want them to do it. To begin you will need a job description. Daydream for a moment and think about the perfect hire for your office. What are they doing? How are they approaching their work? What are they achieving? What do they know? What is their background? Make your vision clear and vivid. You will need to put this information in a job description along with specific performance expectations for each major area of responsibility. For example, if you want to hire an assistant/bookkeeper, what would they do? Perhaps they would answer the phone, schedule appointments, troubleshoot customer problems, track sales, invoice customers, and pay bills. With each function, define specific performance expectations.

Table 1

MAJOR RESPONSIBILITY AREAS	PERFORMANCE EXPECTATIONS
Answer the phone	All callers feel a warm, welcoming, professional person who happily assists them with their needs; takes time to really understand their needs or questions; and willingly goes above and beyond to provide answers or resolve their problem. It is a pleasure speaking with this employee. It is always a positive customer experience. For twenty years, I have been calling StarOne Federal Credit Union and I feel this way after every phone call.
Schedule appointments	Appointments are scheduled with care and precision according to the manager's specific direction and guidance. Provides reminders and heads up anticipating problems or issues. Proactively resolves meeting conflicts in a positive, professional manner. All parties involved in schedule conflict are satisfied with the outcome.
Trouble shooting customer problems	Listens and seeks to understand customer problems and points of view. Lets the customer voice concern without interruption. Customer feels acknowledged and heard. Asks questions to identify the problem. Identifies a solution. Fixes the problem and follows up to ensure customer concern was addressed in a positive, professional manner.

MAJOR RESPONSIBILITY AREAS	PERFORMANCE EXPECTATIONS
Track sales	Sales are tracked with 100% accuracy. Identifies trends and anomalies and reports them to manager with thoughtful insight and recommendations. Tracks sales to monthly and annual goals and against prior three-to-five year performance. Suggests ways to increase sales and meet sales goals.
Invoice customers (Accounts receivable)	Invoices are 100% accurate. They are tracked, monitored, and followed up on in a positive, professional manner. If anything appears off on the invoice, employee checks with manager before sending it. Takes proactive steps to resolve issues before they become a problem.
Pay bills (Accounts payable)	Bills are accurately coded, tracked, and paid on time. Accounts payable is monitored in relation to budget and cash flow, and trends and anomalies are reported to manager with thoughtful insight and recommendations.

Once you know what you want your new employee to do, determine the skills necessary to perform that job. In the example above, the candidate will need social fluency and high attention to detail. Let's take a closer look at the specific technical and performance skills that align with our job description. These skills will become the selection criteria.

Table 2

Technical Skills	Performance Skills
1. Scheduling using Outlook 2. Tracking sales on Salesforce 3. Proficient in Microsoft Office: Word, Excel, PowerPoint 4. Sales forecasting 5. Accounts payable 6. Accounts receivable	1. Strong interpersonal communication skills 2. Customer service skills 3. High attention to detail 4. Managing multiple priorities 5. Self-directed

The selection criteria drive the structure of the interview process. To select an exceptional person, you will want to include multiple assessment opportunities specific to the job you are hiring. For the assistant/bookkeeper, you might:

a. Have multiple interviews using behavior based, open-ended questions asking for specific examples of their past experience.

b. Perform skills assessments: e.g. go into Salesforce, post abc, and run xyz report.

c. Role-play a customer problem, or have the candidate respond to a customer problem in writing

d. Use a behavior assessment tool, such as the Predictive Index, which reveals a candidate's natural preferences and strengths they bring to a job.

When hiring a junior designer, you might perform a behavior based interview, a portfolio review, a skills assessment specific to design work, a new customer role-play, and a behavior assessment. This selection process allows you to learn about what the candidate has done in the past, to assess what they can do in the moment, and to gain insight into their work style and strengths.

A multifaceted interview process provides a rich source of data for you to use in selecting an exceptional person. It also allows the candidate to see if this job, company, and supervisor work for them. It is a positive experience for all parties. Exceptional people appreciate a thorough interview process that accentuates their natural skills and abilities. Multiple interviews enable you to gauge the candidate's timeliness, professionalism, and demeanor. They also provide the candidate with greater insight into the culture, you (the leader), and the organization.

The final step in hiring is to conduct an objective rating of each candidate. See example below.

Table 3: Candidate Rating Sheet

Rate candidate on 1 - 5 scale.

(1) Unsatisfactory, (2) Less than acceptable, (3) Average/Competent, (4) Above average; (5) Exceptional

Skills Evaluated	First Interview	Second Interview	Third Interview	Final Evaluation
Technical Skills:				
Scheduling				
Microsoft Office: Word, Excel, PowerPoint				
Sales tracking and forecasting				
Accounts payable				

Skills Evaluated	First Interview	Second Interview	Third Interview	Final Evaluation
Accounts receivable				
Performance Skills:				
Interpersonal skills				
Customer service				
Attention to detail				
Managing multiple priorities				
Self-directed				
Organizational fit with company culture and values				
Summary comments				

A global telecommunications company was launching a new product and wanted to hire an exceptional product manager. I worked with the hiring team to identify the job duties, selection criteria, selection process, and to develop the rating sheet. After a full day of interviewing their top candidates the six-person interview team assembled to discuss the candidates, and make their selection. As I entered the room there was a very light, upbeat, jovial atmosphere. One of the interviewers was telling a story about one of the candidates that he had worked with in the past and everyone started to laugh. As we sat down to get started, the hiring manager told me that there was a very positive feeling about one of the candidates who had previously worked with one of the interviewers. Everyone started to chime in about what a nice guy he was and how they felt he would fit in nicely with the team. I told them I was glad they found Mr. Delaware to be a nice guy and a good fit. I then suggested that we all take out the rating sheet and rate each candidate on the selection criteria we had all agreed was essential to hiring an exceptional product manager. After reviewing the ratings and discussing each candidates qualifications, Mr. Delaware was not selected for the position. The hiring manager thanked me for guiding the process and keeping them true to the skills they needed for the position. It would have been easy to just hire someone that everyone liked. It can be helpful to have a knowledgeable, objective human resources (HR) professional guide you in this process. HR consultants can assist you in all the steps of hiring with specificity listed below.

- Create job description
- Identify selection criteria (technical, performance skills)
- Determine selection process components
- Conduct multifaceted interview process
- Rate candidates on selection criteria
- Select an exceptional person

2. Articulate the Exceptional

This principle is about getting very, very clear and vivid about what exceptional looks like in a position. For someone to perform at an exceptional level they need to know the target. Take time to write down the job duties, how they should be performed, and the results you expect with each duty. Then, ask the employee what they think exceptional performance looks like in their job and for each of their duties. You want to start by acknowledging the employee's knowledge and experience, and building their confidence. If needed, expand on what the employee shared; redirect, and discuss what you have defined as exceptional. Demonstrate or provide a work sample of what exceptional looks like.

The list of tasks and performance expectations identified in Table 1 provide a starting point for a discussion for the assistant/bookkeeper.

Once you have discussed what exceptional looks like, let the employee know you believe they can perform exceptional work. Acknowledge and recognize exceptional performance when you see it. Employees often wonder if they are doing it right or meeting expectations. Articulating the exceptional positively impacts both the organization and the employee experience. An exceptional employee enjoys coming to work and doing what they know is exceptional performance.

I worked with a national franchisor who owned or serviced hundreds of franchises. There was a small percentage of franchises at the very, very top that were three to four times more productive and profitable than the other franchises. The franchisor decided to go to the very top franchisees and ask them what were they were doing that made them so successful. The franchisor asked me to interview the franchisees and their teams, and to observe the franchisees in action to determine what leadership behaviors made them so successful. What were the behaviors? What did they look like? How would you know that people were doing them? How did these leadership behaviors figure into their daily work? How did they generate productivity and profit? All the top franchisees exhibited thirteen leadership behaviors. A program was designed to teach these thirteen behaviors to a segment of franchisees that were not in the top tier. After training, these franchisees achieved a twenty-nine percent higher gross margin than the company average, and generated thirty million dollars of gross revenue above the company average. What's interesting about this example is that the franchisor had previously established specific activities and metrics for franchisees to hit it to be successful. They had not, however, articulated "how" to perform those activities. The thirteen leadership behaviors related to daily execution. That is an example of how clear and specific guidance about what exceptional looks like, will lead to quantifiable business results. Both the franchisees and the franchisor benefited.

3. Train Thoroughly

Train one person thoroughly. The key word is thoroughly. The problem with most training is that owners and organizations put together a training program and they think that when the training program is finished the employee is trained. That is not necessarily true. When the training is over, the only thing certain is that the training is over. It doesn't mean that the employee knows exactly how to do the job. Train until you see the job being performed effectively and the results meet your expectations. The extra time invested in thorough training, using effective training methods, will pay off with an exceptional employee who is competent and committed. Many exceptional employees blossom after thorough training. Companies I work with continue to rave about the results of thorough training.

I knew a highly enthusiastic, high energy, results oriented sales person. He had previous sales experience in another industry and the hiring company had high hopes for his success. During the interview process, everyone thought he was going to be the next top sales person. After three months on the job, he was not meeting his sales targets. The employee went through the training program and had the background, skills, and experience to do the job. Why wasn't he meeting the minimum sales targets? When they asked the employee what support he needed the employee said, "I am not comfortable and confident in what I am doing. I still don't know if I am doing the job right." The company realized that the employee had not received enough training to be competent. The corporate training director spent one week training him in hopes that he would then be able to hit the sales targets. During that week, the trainer sat at the employee's desk, helped him organize and prioritize his work, demonstrated how to make effective sales calls, listened to the employee make calls, and gave him feedback. As a result, the man focused on the sales activities that produce results. His sales calls became more and more effective, and he started to relax and enjoy his calls. He started to make sales and exceeded the monthly sales target. Over the next nine months this man's performance and production skyrocketed. He went on to achieve President's Club despite his slow start. Not only did he become an exceptional sales person, but he also became an exceptional sales manager and regional manager. He was always exceptional; he just needed more thorough training to achieve his full potential.

If your training method is more or less to tell your employees to read the manual, watch the video, and hit the ground running, your odds of exceptional employee performance are low. Thorough training includes: 1) State the purpose and goal of the task; 2) Take time to ask the employee about their knowledge and experience related to the task, including what they have done before; 3) Demonstrate or illustrate what a good job looks like; 4) Have trainee perform the job and receive feedback on the job; 5) Keep working closely with the employee and coach them until they become competent, and you see them perform the job in an effective manner, achieving the desired results.

Now that you have hired and trained an exceptional employee, care and feeding come into play. You can hire someone exceptional, but if you don't continue to nurture them, they will not flourish or stay. The next eight principles focus on how to cultivate an exceptional employee. If you have an exceptional employee on staff, employ these principles and they will thrive. If you have multiple employees, apply these principles to one person first. Then you can add more after you have mastered the principles with one exceptional employee.

4. Honor Employee with One-on-One Meetings

Honor your employee by conducting one-on-one employee focused meetings. This meeting is for them. They are the priority topic of the meeting. Ask questions such as: How are you doing? Are you enjoying your job? What do you need help in? How can I support you in being successful? After your personal conversation about how they are doing and where they are at, review their performance, production, and provide feedback and coaching. This meeting demonstrates the employee's importance and value. You are there to help and support them in being successful. Meetings should be private and uninterrupted. Avoid rescheduling or cancelling meetings. The key is to honor the employee.

Sally was super excited for her one-on-one meetings with her supervisor Cindy. It was a coveted time that Sally highly enjoyed. Sally left those meetings invigorated, inspired, focused, and committed. No matter what state of mind Sally went into the meeting with, she left uplifted. Cindy never canceled, rescheduled, or was late for one of her one-on-one meetings. Cindy focused on Sally and how she could support her in being successful. All Cindy's meetings started the same way: How are you doing? How are you feeling about your job? How are you feeling about your performance? Then she just listened. Sally knew she could give Cindy an honest answer. That was one benefit of the meetings. They were open and candid. There were laughs, tears, role-plays, training, and coaching. Sally felt honored, valued, important, and knew Cindy believed in her. Sally flourished under Cindy's leadership. Cindy was known throughout the company as an exceptional manager with exceptional employees. As one of her former employees, I reflect fondly on those one-on-one meetings. Not only did I grow as an employee in my role, but I observed an exceptional leader in action.

5. Adjust Your Leadership Style

There is no one best leadership style for all employees. Neither micromanagement or macromanagement (leaders who tell employees, "come see me if you have a problem or need help") are universally effective leadership styles. By adjusting and calibrating the level of direction and support you provide, based on the employees' skill level, you will increase the employee's performance and well-being. How do you do that? Start by asking your employee about their knowledge, experience, and comfort level with a specific task. Then discuss the amount of leadership direction and support they will need to be successful. Together agree on a style that supports them in accomplishing the goal. For example, you may have a designer who is fully competent at bidding and tracking the costs on projects from fifty-thousand dollars to a quarter-million dollars. However, on a three-million-dollar project, that designer may need additional support, direction, and resources to bid and track the project. Thus, adjust your leadership style to be more instructive and supportive. I highly recommend The Ken Blanchard Companies Situational Leadership®II Workshop to leaders who want to become fully competent in adjusting their leadership style to best support their employees.

6. Leverage Employee Preferences

Your employee has natural communication and workstyle preferences. A behavior assessment tool such as the Myers-Briggs Type Indicator, DISC, or Predictive Index will reveal them. After you and your employee take the assessment and debrief the results, you can better understand each other's communication and work style and work more easily and cooperatively together. By appreciating and embracing your employee's natural style, you will capitalize on their strengths and will increase productivity and the employee's well-being. I had a remote employee who was exceptionally creative and accurate in her work. With little direction, she designed amazing training and marketing materials. She also produced twenty-to-thirty page statistical reports with zero errors over the fifteen years I worked with her. When we first started working together, I would call her up and explain her task over the phone informally. That was my natural, extroverted style. I felt it was fast and efficient for me to do it that way.

Early in our work together, she asked if I could email her assignments and she would call if she had questions. At first, I felt a bit put off. Then I decided to give it a try. Putting my assignment instructions in writing forced me to be clearer about the specification and expectations. It reduced the number of revisions that occurred with verbal instructions. The employee produced exceptional work that exceeded my expectations every time. We have recently talked about this and she said she probably would have quit if we did not change the assignment format because it was difficult and frustrating for her to decipher my big picture, verbal instructions. She was not comfortable with that style of instruction. Her behavior profile revealed she was a very quiet, methodical, thorough, detail-oriented person. She liked working independently within her areas of expertise to assure high-quality, by-the-book results. She enjoyed stability and predictability in her work environment and responsibilities. She preferred emails as a positive, nonthreatening approach when it was necessary to correct, change, or criticize her work. The comfort and predictability of specific and detailed email instructions and clarifications played to her strengths. She paid attention to the instructions and delivered with 100 percent accuracy and always exceeded the expectations by giving more. As her manager, I would sing her praise in emails after each client engagement that I utilized her work product. It made her smile and feel good knowing her job was well done. After fifteen years of working together it has been a fruitful, positive relationship for both of us. Sometimes adjusting your style will keep an exceptional employee and sometimes adjusting your style will create an exceptional employee. In this case, it did both.

7. Coach for Nourishment

Do you see yourself as a coach? Do your actions inspire your employee to set their sights high, take bold action, be the greatest version of themselves, and achieve more than they thought was possible? If not, they can. When your employee is being the greatest version of themselvesves, they perform at their highest level and achieve extraordinary results. You have one person to coach to exceptional performance. Start with assessing their skills. Take time to watch and observe them at work. See them in action and identify their strengths and development areas. Give positive and constructive feedback in the moment so it is clear and easy to understand what behaviors to continue, start doing and stop doing. Provide skill training that strengthens, enhances, and expands their strengths and develops skills that are not fully developed to a level of competence. Role modeling, role-playing, training, and coaching will develop and strengthen your employee's skills. Your encouragement, belief in their ability to succeed, and trust will nourish the employee. Your coaching provides sustenance like sunshine and water to a plant. It will make your employee stronger, more confident, and committed. When an employee sees you as a coach (someone who knows them, values them, and appreciates them, sees them as high potential, and works with them to be their best) they are energized to perform at an exceptional level. Challenge and stretch your employee to achieve more than they thought possible. Encourage them and let them know you believe in them, trust them, and support them to take action and make decisions. Highlight the skills and good judgement they have exhibited on the job. When they err, let them know it is all part of the process of growing and getting better. It is part of the growth process. The knowledge and experienced gained will make them more effective in the future. With your coaching, they will flourish and grow.

Michael is an exceptional coach admired for his business acumen, political savvy, and honest communication. His feedback was delivered with warmth and a genuine desire to make the employee more effective in their role. His coaching enhanced employees skills and helped them perform at a higher level. After a client meeting that did not go as well as hoped, Michael asked Kim how she felt about the meeting. She told him she was frustrated and disappointed that the client did not choose the proven-best practice methodology that they both knew worked exceptionally well. Michael acknowledged and agreed that the approach had a strong track record of success with organizations. He asked Kim what she thought the client felt during the meeting. She told Michael that the client seemed steadfast in his approach. Michael asked Kim if she was aware that she pitched this proven methodology three times throughout the meeting. She had not realized how many times she pitched it. She felt passionate about the method and was hoping the rationale would persuade the client. Instead, the client got annoyed. Michael empathized, and also stated that the client felt strongly about his own ideas and approach. Kim asked Michael what she could do differently to be more effective. He told her to gather information from the client regarding their needs, ideas, and parameters first. Listen keenly and consider the client's thoughts and situation. Then, fully informed, make one compelling, persuasive recommendation. Michael role modeled how to do this. He also role-played with Kim and coached her on how to make one strategic presentation to a client. Kim felt acknowledged, empathized, grateful for the feedback. The coaching enabled her to grow and develop. Kim made more effective recommendations.

8. Applaud Generously

Go out of your way to acknowledge, recognize, and reward exceptional performance. When you acknowledge your employees' performance, let them know they are important and valued members of the team as well as integral to the success of the organization. Harvard Business School research shows that praising employees boosts productivity, increases creativity, and reduces stress on the job. Praise reinforces positive behavior and expresses gratitude and appreciation. Praise is free. It requires little effort. It makes employees feel good and in many cases, work harder. Generously applaud exceptional performance.

Resource: https://www.forbes.com/sites/christophernelson/2015/11/01/ latest-research-says-praising-employees-boosts-productivity-after-all/ - 776f16b55f80

9. Propel Performance

Periodic performance conversations can powerfully catapult performance to new and higher levels. These conversations include both a review of performance and employee development and coaching. Together examine the employee's performance in relation to goals, metrics, and standards. Start the conversation seeking to understand how the employee sees their performance. What do they think they are doing well? What do they think they can improve on?

One business owner propelled my performance quarterly by asking: What is one thing that if you improved would positively impact your production and company results? I would give him an answer and we would discuss it. Many times, we agreed to work on something different than what I suggested. That was part of the learning process. He committed to work with me to develop that skill and I agreed to focus on it and make positive improvement. Each quarter I became more proficient in a specific skill that directly impacted the business. I grew tremendously in my skill and business acumen. The company, in turn, obtained higher productivity and greater business results. I was dedicated and committed to this owner. Working for him brought enormous job satisfaction. I am eternally grateful.

10. Lead with Kindness

Make a conscious choice, moment-by-moment, to slow down and be kind in words and actions to your employee. Emma Seppala, Ph. D, a researcher at Stanford University, states that "being a kind boss pays off." Research indicates that leaders who project warmth and kindness are more effective than those who lead with toughness. The reasons include that the employee feels greater trust with someone who is kind. In turn, they are more loyal, they apply discretionary effort, and they are more likely to go out of their way to be helpful and friendly to other employees. Results of being kind include: improved customer service, employee well-being, employee productivity, and enhanced health. Positivity is sustenance for your exceptional employee. Kindness is good for both your souls. *Resources: http://www.incourageleading.com/ lead-with-kindness-youll-get-better-results/* and Hard Data on Being A Nice Boss, at Harvard Business Review.)

11. Demonstrate You Care

Genuine care is the secret sauce to keeping an exceptional employee. It is showing real interest and concern for the well-being of your employee. What does that look like? It could be as simple as making time to answer a question; listening with your full attention, with no cell phone in sight; truly seeking to understand the employees point of view; spontaneously checking in with an employee to see how they are doing; honoring your commitments to your employee (e.g., completing a task you told them you would do, showing up on time and prepared at meetings, supporting them in a meeting; noticing when something is wrong or that your employee is not being themselves and asking why; or taking five minutes to chat. Taking simple actions that show genuine care for the well-being of your employees can have a powerful impact. Employees want to work for managers they trust, respect, and who care. Research has proven that employees who feel cared about provide higher productivity, better customer service, and are cooperative, helpful team members. The Walt Disney Company is dedicated to nurturing and developing a culture of care. Disney Institute trains their leaders to find as many ways as practically possible to regularly demonstrate genuine care for their people. Two resources you may want to check out are *https:// www.disneyinstitute.com/blog/a-disney-leaders-perspective-creating-a-culture-of-care/* and *https://www.disneyinstitute.com/blog/four-ways-to-consistently-demonstrate-genuine-care/*

You know what it takes to lead one person well. That one employee will be extraordinary. Put these principles into action one person at a time. These pivotal management practices will integrate into the exceptional leader you are. Then, leading two, three, four, or even ten exceptional people will be your superpower!

I am not going to sugarcoat this: this process, when done correctly, in the way Eileen describes, is a true example of "do not mistake simple for easy."

When you read this chapter, I'm sure throughout most of it, you thought, "Sure, that makes sense," or "Yes, I kind of do that now." If you are already doing some of these things, then high five! At least you are giving your process for team development and management consideration. However, at the risk of being too blunt, I truly doubt that even five percent of small business owners are executing the team-building process with the level of care and attention that Eileen advises us to.

We have had the great privilege and benefit of Eileen's coaching as we have built our team at Window Works. Frankly, when you do it right, it is daunting. For our most recent hire, completing just step one, with intention and focus, required three, two-hour coaching sessions!

Ah, but the result was magical. By taking the time to identify with specificity the job description, the responsibilities, the technical skills, and the performance expectations of the ideal candidate, our job posting attracted the right people like the Pied Piper attracted the townspeople's children. Once we had a pool of potential candidates, we continued with Eileen's advice in step one when qualifying the candidates, interviewing them, and evaluating them. Her proven process easily narrowed a wide selection of job seekers to the one whom we ultimately invited to join our team.

Our work with this hire, as well as our current employees, continues now as we follow Eileen's remaining ten steps to ensure that Window Works is a company of exceptional employees, one at a time.

Because of her process, we now have an exceptional team, and we have set our sights on significant growth for 2019. Together, we are all after our goals, and we are taking no prisoners! We are confident that the money and energy we spend to build our business can be handled exceptionally, guaranteeing the return on our investment. You can do the same. You should do the same. Build your team with purpose and direction, and together you will grow your business to new heights, reaching goals you might have never imagined.

- LN

About the Author

Eileen Hahn is a leadership consultant who works with firms like Anheuser-Busch, Ericson Worldwide, General Motors, Legoland, and the San Diego Padres, as well as smaller entrepreneurial firms. She teaches the executives in these organizations how to hire and lead exceptional employees who bring fire and energy to their work, achieve high levels of performance, and generate financial results.

Eileen appeared on LuAnn's podcast, episode 363:

https://luannnigara.com/363-power-talk-friday-eileen-hahn-building-an-exceptional-interior-design-team/

Section Three

Building Your Pipeline

CHAPTER 8

Fred Berns

During the first few months of the podcast, I was constantly on the hunt for guests, particularly recognized experts in the industry. One day, on yet another internet search, I typed: "Interior design business coach." Fred Berns was at the top of the list. Soon I would come to know how well-deserved that top ranking on Google was.

I remember emailing Fred and inviting him to be on the show. He was immediately interested, and I was thrilled. By the time I interviewed Fred the first time, I had already completed my first dozen or so interviews. Interviewing Fred was different. Fred has spent years analyzing the business side of interior design. He has taken the time to compare and look for the commonalities among successful designers and the also the commonalities among designers who are not successful. This is smart because both sides reveal useful information. The result is that Fred has created a body of work that is clear, concise, and indisputable.

The first time that I interviewed Fred, it was not like the other interviews that featured mostly amiable conversation, led by my questions and curiosity. Not a chance. Fred emailed me a few days before with a specific a topic that included a detailed list of tips he wanted to be sure to share and to teach. During the interview, he talked, and I scribbled like crazy.

Three years and eight episodes later, Fred always delivers on the promise of that Google search. Without a doubt, we hit the jackpot when I found Fred.

I have come to expect four things from every episode with Fred (and this chapter is exactly the same):

- *It will be jam-packed with ideas.*
- *It will be extremely well thought out.*
- *It will include specific strategies to grow your business.*
- *These strategies are ones you can execute yourself if you prefer not to hire an expert.*

In this chapter, you will learn about "looking the part" when attracting the higher-end client. It's not about having the right pocketbook on your arm. Instead it is about your messaging, it's about your marketing, and it's about knowing yourself and your value. Fred knows this better than most anyone in the industry.

- LN

Proven Marketing Strategies that Attract Luxury Clients
By Fred Berns

So many interior designers work so hard to connect with luxury level clients, but too few succeed. Why?

It's a question I've pondered often during my thirty-year career coaching and creating promotional copy for design professionals worldwide. It's taken a while, but I've finally come up with an answer: Most designers don't attract luxury because they don't *look like* luxury.

Sure, many have extravagant images in their portfolios. They may carry a few luxury product lines. They may even attempt to *play the part* of a luxury designer. But they simply don't look the part.

The problem is in their promotion. Many do a poor job of marketing themselves as high-end designers. They don't dramatically differentiate themselves from the legions of other designers trying to tap into the high-end marketplace. In fact, they undersell and undervalue themselves. As a result, they fail to attract the clients they want and deserve.

If your interior design business isn't where it could be, or should be, that likely has nothing to do with your design expertise or lack thereof. Or your competition. Or the local economy. It may have everything to do with you. Chances are, you're getting in your own way, blocking your own progress by not blowing your horn, tooting your flute, and marketing yourself as a uniquely qualified, luxury-level design professional.

The problem is that competition has never been keener. Never has it been easier to get elsewhere the design services and products that you sell. Do a Google search for "Interior Designers Denver," for example, and you come up with nearly 1,700,000 listings in a nanosecond.

Given those kinds of numbers, why should clients hire you? What makes you different?

How well you answer that question will determine how successful you are at cracking the luxury market.

One word can help you set yourself apart, make an instant impact, and leave a lasting impression. The word is your ultimate differentiator, your fee and price justifier, your "buzz" builder and your brand.

That word is "only."

Are you the *only* design professional in your area who offers a certain service? Are you the *only* one who carries a particular product line? Are you the *only* one who specializes in serving the high-end client niche?

Tell them what only you do, and they'll work only with you.

"Only" is your million-dollar marketing word. Your "only" statement is your YOU-nique Selling Proposition and your phrase that pays.

My *Big Splash, Little Cash Marketing Manual* (whatsyouronly.com/interior-design-business/big-splash-little-cash-marketing-materials-manual) contains several examples of these phrases. Here are some of them:

- ... the region's only award-winning interior architectural firm specializing in green and universal design.
- ... the only award-winning firm in Canada with over forty professionals dedicated solely to interior design.
- ... Florida's only interior designer focusing on residential and commercial design of spaces used by children.
- ... the area's only real estate stager with a degree in landscape architecture.
- ... the state's only LEED-certified design and architecture company.
- ... the only window fashion professional in Mexico City specializing in assisted living facilities.
- ... the only company providing Teknion office furniture in Milwaukee.
- ... the only company that designs country clubs and spas throughout the Southeast.

"Only" is the best, but not the *only*, winning word you can use to position yourself in the luxury arena. In my Victory Vocabulary (whatsyouronly.com/interior-design-business/victory-vocabulary), I list seventy-five such words, including: first, newest, latest, oldest (longest-established), largest, and award-winning.

Those who are most successful in connecting with luxury-level clients realize that, first and foremost, they're not selling furniture, fabrics, or Formica. They understand that, first and foremost, they're selling themselves. They're outstanding *personal* salespeople.

The good news about personal marketing is that some of the most powerful promotion costs the least.

Getting quoted and promoted online and in the media is low-cost, high-impact marketing at its best. You can take advantage of free publicity, the best advertising that prominent design professionals *can't* buy.

Gain visibility, credibility, and a competitive edge by submitting news releases to area online and traditional media outlets every time you sign a major client, add a luxury product line, win an award, launch a blog or podcast, speak at a key industry conference, celebrate an anniversary in your business, or achieve some other milestone. Connect with online, print, and broadcast media and offer yourself as a "resource" about everything having to do with high-end residential and commercial design. Create a media "hit list" of those outlets that target your best prospects. Develop a database of bloggers, reporters, editors, TV and video producers, and others who follow the design industry and inform them of your willingness to help anytime they need information or an interview resource.

Once you get in touch, stay in touch: update them regularly on what's now, what's news, what's in, what's out, what's hot, and what's not.

Get over this idea that those who report on the interiors industry in your region are doing *you* a favor when they use your comments in their broadcasts, podcasts, blog posts, articles, or other channels. In fact, you are doing *them* a favor by sharing your insights and expertise.

It's a win-win relationship. You get interviewed and featured in strategic media outlets. Journalists and others gain access to an invaluable industry authority: you. The media needs you and your industry insights to lend credibility to their shows, articles, and posts as much as you need them to help promote yourself and your company.

My greatest challenge, in my former career as a print and broadcast journalist, was to find sources that I could regularly pose questions to and quote in my reports. Consider this: every month, every week and, in some cases, every day, those professionals have to fill space or air time. By supplying them with timely information, you offer a service they want and badly need.

You need not be a Pulitzer Prize-winning journalist to develop content for the media. The key is to be able to share tips, trends, and techniques in an interesting, non-technical way and to address the biggest changes or challenges or hottest innovations in your industry.

Timing is everything: the more you can relate your information to stories in the news today, such as a seasonal event or the recent heat wave or a downturn in the local economy, the better your chances are of getting your story published or aired.

An advantage of articles over social media is their shelf life. While a tweet may disappear within seconds, a column or blog post has a much more lasting impact. A prospect may come across your article and contact you days, months, or even years after you created it.

In addition, articles by or about you lend you far more credibility than paid advertisements or commercials. Business owners can save a great deal of money and gain more visibility by focusing their marketing efforts on developing content for, rather than advertising in, the media. Position yourself as *the* source of information for high-end design in your area. Talk, tweet, text, and post about what's new, now, and neat in your marketplace.

Public speaking is a good way for design professionals to create credibility and establish expertise and get high-caliber clients and projects. Designers can share their insights by speaking at home shows, facility manager conferences, lunch and learn meetings for realtors, continuing education classes, or other public programs. It's an easy way to make a big splash for little cash.

More and more design pros are offering seminars, courses, clinics, workshops, and other programs as a way to get name recognition and build their client base and bottom line. Then again, you can always stage your own event. Years ago, a Denver-area luxury designer landed a remodeling job worth more than $400,000 from one of her "Quick Fix Remodeling Tips" seminars.

Speaking to a group of potential customers is powerful promotion as its best. Teach 'em what you know—and watch your business grow. Some tips on how to add class to your class and book a bunch of business while you're at it:

Team Up—Ask a retailer, vendor, supplier or other "partner" to promote and host your program. Point out that it's a great way for them to reach out to their target audience.

Touch 'em with your Topic—Focus on a subject you know about and your affluent prospects care about. Fine art and sculpture, bathroom glitz and glamour, wine cellars, media rooms, terrific technology: the possibilities are endless.

Touch 'em with your Title—Choose a program name that catches their fancy and attention. Examples: "Preparing Your Luxury Home for Resale; "What's Hot & Not in High End Window Fashions;" "Turn Your House into a Home for the Holidays."

Make Yourself Memorable—Add pizzazz to your presentation by including humor and anecdotes. Provide top-notch visual aids and handouts.

Make Yourself "Reachable"—Provide complete contact details, links to your website, Houzz and other social media sites, and any other information that makes it as easy for attendees to connect with you.

Sell Yourself—The most important sale is the personal one. Turn your class contacts into contracts by promoting yourself as a uniquely qualified, one-of-a-kind designer.

Focus on the Catalogue, Not Just the Class—Your course description in the right kind of catalogue can bring you lots of business from those who never attend your class. Why? The catalogue may reach hundreds, and the course description positions you as an expert.

Get Their Feedback—Provide a form on which attendees can evaluate your program. Use it to solicit their referrals.

Too many design professionals let their fear of public speaking prevent them from giving presentations. Don't make that mistake. Remember that those who attend your programs don't do so to critique your presentation skills. They come to learn from your expertise about design.

Share key talking points from your presentation with online outlets and local trade publications. Use social media, email, and your website to spread your know-how, and craft clever email signatures and voicemail messages that promote you as well as your services.

Other ways to make a maximum impact for a minimal investment: create and distribute videos, write a blog and/or e-zine, submit articles to online and print media, and build your database though live and social networking.

The best marketing tool with which you can promote yourself to the luxury market is the bio on your website, Houzz site and in social media. There's no better way to introduce yourself and communicate your value than with a stellar personal profile. With it, you can position yourself as a uniquely qualified leader in the local luxury marketplace.

Your bio can do that, but most bios *don't* do that. If yours is like the majority of design industry bios, it undersells you. It may even block you rather than boost you and disqualify rather than qualify you from the kind of projects and clients that you want and need.

Too many bios are vague and wordy, focusing way too much on old certifications and degrees and way too little on recent accomplishments and milestones. All too common are tired old sentences, such as "She's committed to providing the best customer service," and all too rare are benefit phrases: explaining, for example, how you save your clients time, money, and stress.

You can't get good clients with a bad bio.

What does it take to create a personal profile that dramatically differentiates you? Consider these bio boosters:

- An "only" phrase ("____ is the area's only residential designer who ...")
- Awards and other honors
- Design specialties

- Experience
- Accomplishments
- Skills and capabilities
- Other qualifications
- Unique services and products
- Publication history (where/how you've been published)
- Client profile (who you serve and how)
- Resources (vendors, contractors, etc.)
- Affiliations
- Educational background

Three rules of the road to keep in mind as you prepare your online promotional profile:

1. Your design skills don't matter. What matters is how clients *benefit* from them.
2. As you prepare to write your bio, don't dwell on your "don't's." Don't fret about the experience, clients, degrees, certifications and awards that you don't have.
3. Highlight, don't hide, your past. Explain how your present-day clients benefit from the skills you gained from your past employment.

Making your bio meaningful and memorable is critical if you're committed to taking your design business to the next level and beyond. You simply can't afford to undersell yourself and fail to give credit where credit is due. You can't afford to leave money on the table because people don't know all that you do. And you can't afford to be your own, best-kept secret.

Your online bio is more than your most vital and valuable personal promotion tool. It's also your most versatile tool. It can promote you and propel your interior design business in so many ways, in so many formats, via so many media.

Include your bio in the following places:

- The "About Us" section of your website
- Your Houzz profile
- All your social media. Formats will vary from the complete (LinkedIn summary) to the curtailed, as in Twitter (140 words) and Instagram (150)
- Your Google profile
- The "personal profile/describe your channel" section on YouTube
- All communication with prospects
- Your email signature, accessible via a link
- Your brand, elevator speech, and voicemail message
- Quotations of your fees (or raising them)
- Confirmations of initial appointments ("I'm looking forward to our meeting and have attached some background information.")
- Client communication about new services or products
- Joint marketing campaigns in which allied professionals promote you to their database
- All pricing proposals, including bids for commercial projects
- Solicitations for speaking engagements
- Catalogues promoting your seminars, courses, classes, workshops, etc.
- Handouts at your presentations
- Proposals for writing and podcast opportunities
- The "about the author" section of your articles, columns, and blogposts
- Resource material for the media (reporters, writers, producers, bloggers, etc.)
- Group directories (e.g., in the "Find a Designer" section of an ASID website)
- Advice for your personal reference list, so they can more effectively recommend you to others
- Showcases of designer and show houses

- Proposals for corporate partnerships
- Proposals for financial assistance for your design firm

There's no better way to promote the luxury market "star" that you are than with a Killer Bio. Do your bio right, or hire someone else to do it for you, and do it now! When you're ready to revise your bio or craft a new one, I can help. I've written promotional profiles for design professionals from Dallas to Dubai. Contact me for more information at **Fred@FredBerns.com**, or register for my introductory coaching session, the **Bio Briefing** (biobriefing.com).

The best way to showcase your new bio is to include it as an attachment in a letter to everyone you need to know, and who needs to know you. I call this a letter of (re-)introduction, a note informing (or reminding) others, say, about your new focus on the luxury market, and about what else is new and noteworthy about your business and yourself.

The letter, which you transmit through email or traditional mail, is an extraodinary way to connect with those with whom you've lost touch and/or those who are unaware of all that you do or can do. It's also an excellent way to establish, or re-establish, top-of-mind awareness.

The letter, with the bio attached, should go out to your entire database. The list of recipients could include former clients, prospects, vendors and suppliers, design industry bloggers and trade media, and any other movers, shakers, and influencers you know.

Use the letter to explain how your clients will gain from the new technology, additional staff, high-end services, and/or product lines that you've recently added. Point out, for example, how your new software will save them time and money, or how your new online video series will keep them up to date on the latest, hottest luxury design trends.

Another key component of your letter: a call to action. Engage recipients by suggesting that they sign up for your Summer Special, follow and "friend" you, download your new free report, check out your latest blog posts, or visit your revised website.

The reintroduction letter is an economical marketing tool that can benefit you in a wide variety of ways. For starters, it affords you the chance to roll out your luxury market brand. The letter reminds your target audience of your value and educates them about *all* that you can do. It's a simple way for you to reach people at a time when they may, in fact, need your services. If their need is less immediate, it may motivate them to put you on their calendar for the near future.

Finally, it gets your name before ex-clients, a valuable strategy to be sure. Management consultant Peter Drucker estimated that the average company has a one-in-fourteen chance of doing business with a prospect, but a one-in-four chance with a former customer. At the very least, your letter may inspire those one-time customers to refer you to others.

Those design professionals who have successfully transitioned to the luxury market are based in markets large and small, have varying degrees of experience, and run their businesses in a wide variety of ways. But they all implement two basic marketing strategies: 1. They aim high, and 2. They gain and maintain an abundant pipeline.

Aiming high, a requirement for working in the luxury design market, begins with a resolution to bond with the best, and avoid the rest. That means hunting eagles, not turkeys. Make it your mission to connect with prospects who value your services so much that they'll pay any price for them. While you're at it, lose the losers, and fire those who take advantage of you, waste your time, and bellyache over every bill.

Promoting yourself to higher-caliber prospects makes way more sense than reaching out to tiny, troublesome ones. Scrambling to connect with and serve a bunch of smaller customers who are more trouble than they're worth makes no sense. Working with too many of the wrong customers is a formula for failure, if there ever was one. Unfortunately, it's a formula too many design professionals follow too often. Why? Because they say "yes" when they should say "no." They accept small jobs with high-maintenance customers who are more interested in bargain basement prices than fine design. If you're stuck with too many of these bottom feeders, you're fishing in the wrong waters.

Tell me about all your small projects for all your small customers, and I'll tell you to think bigger. I'll tell you to make more profitable use of your time by focusing, instead, on your best clients.

Ask them about a "Phase II" for the current project and about upgrades and updates to their vacation homes as well as their primary residences. Discuss your commercial, as well as residential, design services or vice versa. At the very least, ask them for referrals, and for testimonials for your website, Houzz site, and other marketing channels.

Often, it takes no more effort to catch the kahunas than to mix with the minnows. You'll bond with the best if you act the part (in your service), look the part (in your marketing), and charge the part of a high-caliber interior design professional. If chasing after more customers is your idea of building your design business, then your way is a poor way.

More customers won't help you substantially increase your profits. More clients will. There's a difference, you know.

A customer buys a chair from you. A client hires you for a project. A customer cares only about the lowest price. A client cares about the best solutions to her design problems. With a customer, you close a deal. With a client, you open a relationship. You may only have a "fling" with a customer. You go steady with a client.

Put your best clients under a microscope, and analyze their every need, before searching for new prospects. The long-term value of a client is more than one hundred times the value of a single transaction. Expanding your relationship with your quality clients beats having a quantity of tiny—and perhaps troublesome—ones.

Think big. Think quality, not quantity. Think eagles, not turkeys.

So how do you reach those eagles? That brings us to the second part of the marketing mindset of high-end designers: their respect for the Power of the Pipeline. Top-performing design professionals build their pipelines by devoting an hour or so a day to making business-building contacts.

Pumping up your pipeline is as simple as reaching out every work day, every week to at least ten individuals who can help you build your business. Sounds easy, doesn't it? You'd be surprised how few design professionals follow that simple, yet systemized approach to connecting with the right people. They fail to realize the potential of their pipeline.

Pumping up the pipeline could mean reaching out to clients and suggesting a next phase for their project. Or emailing a former client about doing an upgrade. Or setting up an appointment with a prospect. It could mean talking to that fabric showroom about sponsoring your seminar. Or that window film specialist about doing some joint marketing. Or that building owner about referrals. Consider texting your high-end builder buddy. Or recontacting those luxury market realtors you talked to a while back. Or following up with the property manager you met recently. Maybe it's reconnecting with the sales rep who stopped by the other day, the one who knows everybody. Or checking in to see if that painter you used last time has some leads for you. Or following up on that query about your Houzz images.

Building your pipeline means smiling and dialing, contacting your contacts, working your network, talking to and tweeting and touching ten people. Or more. It means reaching out to everyone and anyone who somehow, in some way, can help you build your business today.

The rationale behind all this is simple: sales is a numbers game. The more contacts you initiate and "touches" you make, the more sales you close. If ever there was a winning strategy to increase your sales, building your pipeline is it. But this winner comes with a warning: it takes work. Hard work.

Making ten contacts a day requires a lot of time and a lot of effort. You'll send lots of emails and texts, and leave lots of phone messages, and, on some days, receive few replies. And get ready for rejection: you'll get plenty of that. You'll get to know "no." But this increased marketing push will also generate a lot more "yeses."

Leading design professionals realize that the path to prosperity and luxury clientele begins with their pipeline. Start building yours, and you'll be astounded at how quickly your sales grow.

By now, you should have a clearer understanding of what it takes to work in the high-end marketplace. At this point, you know the words to use to promote yourself as a uniquely qualified, one-of-a-kind luxury designer. You've learned some strategies with which you can make a maximum impact for a minimal investment of time and money. You have some ideas on how to roll out your luxury service brand by (re-) introducing yourself to those you need to know. And, hopefully, you now understand the importance of aiming high and thinking big as you take your design business to the next level.

But Looking the Part, in and of itself, will be meaningless, if you don't Charge the Part.

One thing may be holding you back from attracting classier clients. That one thing may be blocking you from generating lucrative, long-term projects. It's the same thing that prevents you from earning the income you want and deserve. That one thing isn't luck. It isn't your location. It isn't a competitor. The one thing holding you back is your fees. They are too low to "qualify" you to work in the high-end market.

"WHAT?!!! No way," you say.

Now you're going to tell me that some of the most affluent homeowners in your area are some of the cheapest. You're going to tell me that you get pushback from clients who insist you already charge too much. You're going to tell me that you have to be a celebrity designer to work in the high-end market. And you're going to give me a whole bunch of other reasons—other than fees—that make it impossible for you to work in the luxury marketplace.

When you're done, I'm going to say: "I don't care." You shouldn't either.

Don't give me all the reasons why you *can't* work in the affluent market. Give me all the reasons you can. I'll help you out here:

> You're a multi-talented design professional fully capable of handling everything from project management and space planning to furniture selection and color consultation.
>
> You're a highly skilled interior consultant and problem solver adept at helping clients overcome their most pressing design challenges.
>
> You have extraordinary resources and contractors and vendors and suppliers, not to mention your portfolio: It's terrific.

Now that we've determined that you "look" the part of a luxury market design professional, why don't you charge the part?

Chances are, wealthy prospects are blown away by your qualifications and expertise. But they're puzzled by your prices. After all, these are people who are used to paying top dollar for top-quality services and products. When you quote fees that they consider too low, they get suspicious. They wonder how you could be so good if you're so cheap.

I've coached and created bios and other promotional materials for luxury market designers all over the world. While they differ in many ways, there's one thing they have in common: they charge top dollar for their services.

If you're serious about working with classier clients, you should, too.

Conclusion

In conclusion, connecting with the luxury market need not be a distant dream. It can and will become a reality once you look the part of a luxury-level designer.

Looking the part means differentiating yourself from competitors, defining what ONLY you do. It means developing and distributing a

Killer Bio that spells out your specialness and establishes your expertise. It means (re-)introducing yourself to the high-end market, showcasing your promotion profile, and updating everyone you need to know about what *they* need to know about you.

Looking the part also means sharing your luxury brand by taking advantage of a wide variety of "big splash, little cash" marketing strategies.

Then you reinforce your brand by charging the part of a highly successful and accomplished interior design professional.

The key component of your new business model should be higher fees. Those attach higher value to who you are and what you do. Affluent clients care far more about who you are than about what you charge. You can set and get any fee as long as you can substantially differentiate yourself from competitors who charge less.

Personal promotion is critical to your future in the high-end marketplace. That's because the most important sale you ever make is the *personal* one.

During my interior design industry career, I've discovered that the most financially successful designers aren't necessarily the *best* designers. They haven't always won the most awards and recognition, nor have they been published in the most places, nor do they have the most certifications or awards.

Rather the most financially successful designers are simply the best self-promoters. Now, maybe that isn't right and that's not fair, but that's fact.

Promote yourself as if your business, career and future in the luxury market depend on it.

You know what? They do.

Fred's chapter, like his podcast episodes, are like a breadcrumb trail in a forest. He always presents a clear path to success. The key is the decision to act on his advice. Only you can make that. When I read Fred's chapter,

my mind connected to the dozens of previous podcast guests who, through their stories, support Fred's strategies.

Here are just a few examples:

- *Filling your pipeline. Fred says to "smile and dial." Reach out to ten people each day. All kinds of people, for all kinds of reasons. You might think that's old school or think, "I don't have time for that." Do you remember Candy Scott from Chicago, on episode 279? She told us she "dials for dollars every Friday." And Remya Warrior from episode 266, who gave us her seven-step networking system that she employs every day.*

- *Connect with online, print, and broadcast media. Ren Miller from episode 12, the Editor-in-Chief of Design NJ, told us point blank, "I am always looking for new projects and for new resources for quotes." Amy Flurry, the author of Recipe for Press and Recipe for Press, Designer Edition, from episodes 108 and 323, gave us the exact plan for cultivating these media relationships.*

- *Ask a vendor, retailer, or supplier to partner, host, and promote programs to get you in front of your target client. Shauna Lynn Simon and I discussed this over two episodes, 84 and 102. Additionally, we employ this strategy at Window Works and host monthly lunch and learns for interior designers. This is a tremendous lead generator for us. As a consequence, we are always on the hunt for a colleague who can lead an informative program.*

These are the real-life designers executing the strategies Fred outlines. He's not talking theory; he knows what successful designers do.

Now you do too.

The danger in this chapter, however, is that it contains so much information—literally dozens of ideas for creating new business—that you might not slow down enough to focus and dissect the information.

To utilize Fred's advice fully, you need to break this chapter down into doable steps. It would be too overwhelming to set out to do them all. Find a few that resonate with you and commit to doing them. When done correctly, these are not one-day projects, but, if done correctly, you will grow your business. Then come back to this chapter anytime you feel like business is slowing down. Between Fred's confidence-boosting encouragement and his tactical strategies to earn new clients, this chapter will be the gift that keeps on giving. It contains so much practical advice that with each reading, you will find a new strategy or possibly discover an idea of your own, sparked by his wisdom.

- LN

About the Author

Fred Berns is among the biggest names in the business of interior design. He's a coach who helps design professionals increase profits by promoting themselves. He's a copywriter who creates bios, website and social media content, and promotional materials for industry pros. He's the author of several learning tools for the industry. And he's a speaker who appears at design industry events worldwide.

Fred has appeared on LuAnn's podcast eight times, on episodes 22, 48, 96, 174, 226, 289, 337, and 393:

https://luannnigara.com/22-fred-berns-how-to-create-a-killer-bio/

https://luannnigara.com/48-power-talk-friday-with-fred-berns/

https://luannnigara.com/96-power-talk-friday-fred-berns-selling-methods-of-the-masters/

https://luannnigara.com/174-power-talk-friday-fred-berns-own-your-only-word-tips-to-discover-yours/

https://luannnigara.com/226-power-talk-friday-fred-berns-5-keys-to-a-fabulous-fall/

https://luannnigara.com/289-power-talk-friday-fred-berns-7-habits-of-luxury-interior-designers/

https://luannnigara.com/337-power-talk-friday-fred-berns-set-and-get-higher-fees/

https://luannnigara.com/393-power-talk-friday-fred-berns-12-ways-interior-designers-sabotage-their-business/

CHAPTER 9

Mark McDonough

M ark McDonough of *Tastefully Inspired is what many would call an "idea man." In every conversation with him, his mind races with ideas on marketing, on promotion, and on how to leverage social media. Nearly every phone call we have starts with my favorite line of his, "Okay, hey, so check this out, how about if you tried this ..."*
And the next words are always pure gold.

I found Mark on Instagram in October 2016. I reached out to him by direct message and asked if he would like to be on my show. At the time, I had probably about a thousand followers, while he was well over thirty thousand. When he said yes, I specifically remember looking at Vin and saying, "Give me a high five! Tastefully Inspired just accepted my invite for an interview!"

Little did I know how pivotal that day would be for me on my podcasting journey.

Mark helped me so much for the next year and a half with ideas, suggestions, strategies, and introductions that one day I finally said to him, "Mark, this is crazy. One, two times, you give me advice that was terrific, but this is now feeling very lopsided. You are always helping me. How I can reciprocate?"

Mark said to me the same thing he had said on the podcast eighteen months before, "No, don't say that and don't feel funny. I just want to hang out with people that I like. I like talking with good people and if I can help them, I want to. I like feeling like we're friends who would have a cup of coffee together and toss ideas around."

In nearly three years I have only been in the same room with Mark two times, but every time we talk, it sure does feel like we're friends having coffee together.

Let me introduce you to your new friend, who just happens to be a genius with Instagram strategies.

- LN

Tackling Instagram: Strategies That Produce Results
By Mark McDonough

If I asked you right now, "What's your Instagram account handle?" could you tell me? More importantly, would you tell me, or would you be too embarrassed? Is your IG account something akin to that cluttered junk drawer we all have in our kitchen? Or are you proud of the hard work you've put in to creating a beautiful grid? In today's world, a digital marketing strategy for your interior design business is a must. With how visual the interior design industry is, we all need to bring our A game to the digital table.

Oh, social media. Some days we love scrolling through beautiful feeds, getting inspiration, just champing at the bit to get our next "inspired" post out there. On other days, we feel like tearing our hair out over what to write in that tiny, blindingly white, text box! We think "What photo to post today? One that is beautiful and yet in line with my brand? Colorful or simple? Wait, is that too much green or ... aaacckk!" It's enough to send some of us into a tailspin!

It is absolutely critical to get a branded, reputable presence on various social platforms in order to run your business smoothly. According to several experts, social media marketing is *the process of creating content for each individual social media platform in order to bring about user engagement.* At the end of the day, isn't that what we're after: engagement with future customers? Social media is growing quickly—that's scary, but it doesn't mean you can hide from it. What that means is that you need to get out there, get seen, stop crying about how you hate using it, and just do it.

As an expert in the field of digital marketing, while I have many recommendations to improve your Instagram game, the most important boil down to a list of nine critical tactics. Before I launch into my list, please make sure you have signed up for a business account. Otherwise, you won't get the benefits of insights and analytics. These are the tools that will help you see what works and what doesn't.

1. The Basics

Your Bio. This is your place, your podium, to state who you are, what you sell, and a bit about yourself. If you want to get more followers, they need to know what you're selling and who you are. It's also a good idea to remember, it's all about them, so pay attention to your copy and speak directly to your target audience. Think carefully on what will attract prospective clients and motivate them to follow your account. Don't forget that this is the only place you can include clickable links (for now), so make sure you include your website or the URL where you want to direct them for more information. You can also add hashtags to the bio, so a couple carefully chosen hashtags can also direct people to your profile.

Here are two examples (it will be apparent who not to emulate and who has a great bio):

What exactly is going on here? Is this person serious about Handmade Homewares? I doubt it.

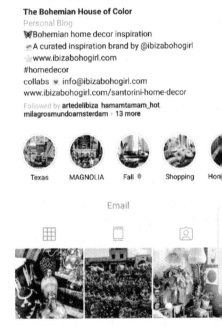

She nailed it! Hashtags, website link, and I know exactly what kind of account I'm following.

Here is your bio checklist:

- Explain who you are and what your business is.
- Use keywords to target your audience.
- Use a link to your website, storefront, Facebook page, and so on.
- Provide a way for people to get in touch with you: include your email address, phone number, or address if you have a physical location.

Be sure your brand is apparent in your grid. You don't want to just throw random pictures out there or people won't have a clue as to what you do. Just refer to the handmade homewares account above. Remember, this is your business account we're talking about, so we don't want to keep seeing what you had for dinner unless you're a food business. You can include a few photos that reflect your personality or share your personal life so that people will know you're a real human, but a little goes a long way.

Always post images and content that resonate with your brand or reflect your business mantra. This means that if you specialize in designing landscapes, then you probably shouldn't be reposting luxury closet spaces. Your followers may get the wrong idea of what you're selling. Kathleen Bandaruk, my sidekick at Tastefully Inspired, put together a great e-book I recommend on creating a killer grid that goes over some of these points. This book is titled *Instagram Grids: Not So Secret and Super Simple Tips for Designers*. It can be downloaded at: http://tastefullyinspired.com/wp-content/uploads/2019/02/Instagram-Grids-for-Designers-Ebook.pdf

Hashtags. Nothing is worse than spending hours thinking through all the cutesy hashtags only to realize that no one is looking for #myhomerenovationprojectsuckedtoday. Do the research and find hashtags that are consistent with your photo and haven't hit the dreaded "ban" list. Many sites offer a lookup tool for banned hashtags that you can use for free.

Get hashtags working for instead of against you! Want one quick tip that will help you save time? Save your frequently used hashtags in your phone's notepad or notebook app. Create a master list together there and copy and paste them in your post. You can put up to thirty hashtags, so use them all wisely, but be sure you rotate them often. Don't use the same ones over and over.

On a side note, also make sure you add a location when you post, because that's another way to show up in the local feeds!

2. Get Busy with Videos, Stories, and the New IGTV Portal

a. **People love videos.** They represent a chance to reach a bigger audience. Once you get used to the medium, find out what works best—maybe you're a Live IG person, or maybe people line up to view your latest project walkthrough on IGTV. Whatever it is, don't be scared of video. It just might prove to be your best friend.

   i. Stories are very powerful and if you have ten thousand followers or more, or are a verified business profile, you have the coveted "swipe-up" feature where you can insert any URL that you want to direct your viewers to.

   ii. Although IGTV is still relatively new, it's the best place to post longer videos, aside from YouTube.

b. **Use the highlights section.** You can save your stories to the highlight section below your profile info. It is a great place to store info on your services, products, or anything else worth mentioning. Some accounts go a step beyond and create a polished look with custom icons for their highlight reels. It's easy to do, and makes you look like a pro. Check out the accounts below:

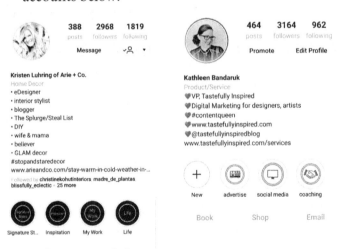

3. Planning Your Posts: What Works, and What Doesn't?

a. **Automatic schedulers.** Getting your content out there in a consistent manner is critical, and using a scheduler is a huge time saver. However, all schedulers are not equal. Some are better for Pinterest and Twitter, while some are better for Instagram and Facebook. Rather than recommending a specific one, I would advise you to do your own research and find out which one works with the social media platforms you use.

A lot of people have asked me, "What time should I post in order to get the most engagement?" As of today, statistics show that 3:00 p.m. on Wednesdays is the best for businesses. Don't ask me why! If you're a business, that is your best bet, but don't neglect all the other times—just maybe post your most relevant post for the week on that day and time.

b. **Editorial calendars.** No matter what scheduler you end up using, you're still going to need to plan out the content: what photo you're using and what copy you want for each post. We use an editorial calendar created by CoSchedule that we share, which not only keeps us organized, but also helps us stay on top of all our social platforms.

4. Creating Graphics

We all know the importance of posting beautiful imagery, but sometimes our photos need a little help. Sometimes, we want to say something to our followers through the image, not just the text box underneath. It's easier than ever to do without an expensive program like Photoshop. Sparkpost, Canva, and PicMonkey are my favorites. In fact, Picmonkey just rolled out a new version to compete with the high-tech photo editing software out there. Just take a look below at what Kathleen did using the new Picmonkey. By adding text and some layers with color, she took an otherwise plain photo (from the free photo service Pixabay) and turned it into an eye-catching graphic with a quote.

We get the question a lot, "What is the best color and filter to use to get engagement?" That has been the subject of many blog posts and articles for years. Some say blue is still the best color to use, but others say that the filter is more important. In fact, Canva did a recent worldwide study that shows that the Clarendon filter is the world's most popular filter. It's no wonder; it brightens, highlights, and makes the colors pop.

5. Staying Consistent and Engaged

This is a hard one, but not staying engaged will set you back and all that hard work you put into creating a following will be in vain. You know your friend who took the summer off to travel the world and you didn't hear from until September? Whether or not she noticed, her IG account suffered. It takes a while to get back in the swing of things and get back in IG's good graces. She will have to post daily if not more than once a day to boost her account again. If you haven't learned anything yet in this chapter, remember this: Post every single day! Consistency is vital for growth.

What about engagement? Instagram loves accounts with comments and more than four words. Posts that just say, "Love it," or "beautiful" don't make the cut. Try to comment on other accounts with comments such as, "I love your wall! What color did you use?" or, "You really hit the nail on the head with this photo!"

Also, turn on your post notifications. A little-known trick to getting organic followers is to be the first in line to comment on large accounts, so go on the account you want to comment on, click the three dots in the top upper right, and choose, "Turn on Post Notifications." Don't forget to comment a full sentence or ask a question back! Interact with them regularly and become one of their favorite commenters or brands! (Hint, hint: turn on post notifications and comment on @tastefullyinspiredblog often and we will get to know and love you!)

If someone comments on your post, please remember to comment back and thank them or respond appropriately. It's important for anyone perusing your posts to see that you are responsive and engaged with your audience.

6. Use the Book (or Action) Button

I have spoken about the importance of connecting a book button on your profile in my podcast and in a video for our Facebook group. I am 100 percent in favor of using it and don't see its importance going away anytime soon. It's a way for customers to buy from you without ever leaving Instagram. Isn't that a no-brainer? Sticking that book button on your account demonstrates:

a. You mean business. You know what you're doing because not everyone has implemented this important tool, and

b. You are making it easy for prospective clients to get in touch with you, book a session or appointment, and complete the purchase!

I can't recommend it highly enough. It takes just a few simple steps to get your own book or action button going.

- First, you need to have a business account. I've already mentioned above how crucial this is to getting insights and data that will help you run your account more effectively.
- Next, if you're using the "Action" button as a booking feature, you need to have an account with Acuity Online Scheduling or Booksy before setting up your IG profile. It's free to sign up and take payment through there, but this needs to be connected to your account first.
- If you aren't a service provider, then you can also use this option to make reservations, order things, or even sell tickets. It's all up to you in how you want to use the feature. It's easily customizable and there are several third-party companies to choose from: Eventbrite or Fandango for tickets, EatStreet or ChowChow for reservations, and so on.
- Next, select, "Edit Profile."
- Tap on your "Contact Options" under "Business Information."
- Tap "Add an Action Button."
- Then select Acuity Scheduling or Booksy if you're using these services to book clients, or, as mentioned above, choose from one of the other third-party vendors according to your need.
- Lastly, add your URL and save.

Voila! Your Book or Action button should be visible and ready to accept business!

Among the many ways to continue boosting your online presence, influencer marketing can get your brand out in front of a bigger audience.

7. Influencer Marketing

If you haven't heard by now, thousands of people are making millions of dollars as paid influencers just to talk about a product. Jaw dropping, I know. Influencer marketing is when you pay an influencer to get the word out on you, your business, or a product. The bottom line is people already follow influencers for a reason: they trust them. If they say something great about you, their viewers are likely to give you a chance and book an appointment or buy your furniture. It's good old-fashioned "word of mouth" in a new and virtual way.

Are you ready to jump in and have Kim Kardashian post a photo of your newest closet design? Be prepared to pay up to a quarter of a million dollars for one post! But it doesn't have to be that way as a bigger following isn't necessarily better. There are three categories of influencers, so pick the one that most resonates with you and fits into your budget.

Macro Influencers are the biggest fish in the pond with followers ranging from two hundred fifty thousand to over a million. The potential reach is huge, but that wide range can also come with much lower engagement and much higher costs.

Power Middle Influencers like Tastefully Inspired have followers numbering between ten and two hundred fifty thousand. They tend to have a better success rate at true engagement with a much more palatable price tag to get you the brand recognition you are looking for. They usually have experience working with reputable brands (see our Tastefully Inspired collaborations with Lamps Plus and Baker Furniture to get an idea of some of the types of promotion we give our partners) with proven results.

Micro Influencers are accounts with fewer than ten thousand followers and typically have good engagement. However, make sure you're looking for an account within your own or a compatible niche, or often it will fall on deaf ears.

Having been in marketing for the last twenty years, I have assembled a team of amazing experts for our company, Tastefully Inspired, to help grow businesses across the globe in our industry. Tastefully Inspired prides itself on being a polished, professional, yet scrappy company, able to cater to any size business that is ready to bring it to the next level and crush the competition. If you have any questions about this chapter, call me today.

❖ ❖ ❖

Mark's nine strategies hit all the bases, from setting up your account to utilizing IG Live and IG stories. The one thing I will add is to be clear on why you are using Instagram. If it is because "all the designers" are on Instagram, that's not quite going to cut it.

An effective Instagram strategy, one that follows Mark's advice, takes time. Time every. Darn. Day. Instagram is like a houseplant: you can water it, talk to it, feed it, and keep it well-loved for months, coaxing it to grow, but ignore it for a few weeks and it's over. Deadville.

I have spoken with many designers with clients who have found them on Instagram, yet I also know designers who have never gained a single client from Instagram.

It comes down to two things.

First, if you like Instagram, whether it brings business in or not, then by all means, spend time relaxing there and enjoy the scenery. This does not mean spending hours during the day pretending you are "marketing." If you enjoy it, do it in your free time as a pleasant diversion.

Second, you must know your target client. If your ideal client is a woman under forty, then odds are, Instagram is a very good place for you to invest your business time and energy. No fooling yourself with this though, okay? What if your ideal clients are typically middle-aged and mostly male? Maybe you cater to affluent bachelors, or C-Suite executives. Are they likely to be found on Instagram? Not in droves.

Does this mean you shouldn't have an IG account? Absolutely not. Your IG account can be a place to send prospective clients once they have found you to see your work, your style, and your personality. Your IG could be something you enjoy, and your IG account could be where you connect with our design community. It's probably just not the major source of your pipeline and, therefore, is probably not the right place to spend hours cultivating a following.

Like everything else in your business, be intentional. Know why you are doing what you are doing.

If Instagram is a big yes for you, then please start at the beginning of Mark's list, working your way through creating an Instagram account that will work for you and benefit your business.

For more advice and insights on Instagram, to sharpen your skills and to stay on top of the latest tips and trends, be sure to listen to Mark's podcast, Tastefully Inspired. He is right there. Grab your coffee and visit a while with him. When you do, listen for when he says, "Hey, check this out ..." As soon as you hear that, perk up your ears!

- LN

About the Author

With over twenty years of marketing expertise, Mark brings his talent to the digital world. He has worked building the brands of many of our industry's most iconic designers. Mark has also collaborated with leading manufacturer's such as Restoration Hardware, Global Views, Studio A Home and Rocky Mountain Hardware, to name a few.

Mark appeared on LuAnn's podcast, episode 110:

https://luannnigara.com/110-mark-mcdonough-founder-editor-of-tastefully-inspired-blog/

CHAPTER 10

Shauna Lynn Simon

I n 2016, Shauna Lynn Simon emailed me, telling me how much she enjoyed listening to my show and that she would love to discuss with me the differences between interior design and home staging. As I had very recently worked with Leah Gomberg, the owner of Sweet Life by Design in Maplewood, NJ, to help sell our home, I thought to myself, "Are design and home staging different enough to warrant an entire show?" Skeptical, but always curious, I scheduled the interview.

My first thought after interviewing Shauna Lynn was, poor Leah, I had been the worst client ever. I had insisted on applying design principles rather than staging principles throughout the process. All I can say is, "Leah, I'm sorry. I really made your job much more difficult than it should have been."

In talking with Shauna Lynn, I recalled how in conversation after conversation, I pushed back on Leah's well-made suggestions (in particular about the furniture placement in my family room). Leah moved it to create traffic flow, but I kept saying but you can't see the yard like this ... yikes. You see, Leah knew what Shauna Lynn describes in her chapter: home staging is redesign for selling, not redesign for living. The two are very different. To be a successful home stager (or a successful home staging client), you have to grasp the fundamental difference. I thought Leah and I simply had different taste, but instead I was redesigning for living, while Leah was redesigning for selling.

Which, of course, it did. Thank you, Leah.

Shauna Lynn also explains the pros and cons to consider in this business model. If you have considered becoming a home stager or if you have wondered if you should add home staging to your ladder of services, this chapter is right for you.

- LN

Home Staging for the Interior Designer
By Shauna Lynn Simon

Now that you have cracked the code on the design world, you might be thinking that it is time to challenge yourself further in order to provide your clients with additional opportunities to work with you. If so, then home staging just might be the answer that you are looking for.

The term "home staging" has been around for decades. While it has grown in popularity over the past 10 years, thanks in part to popular television shows, it can be traced back more than 40 years. While home staging is not a regulated industry, meaning that there are no official training standards, home staging has its own trade association and conventions, and is touted by top real estate agents as an essential home-selling tool.

When I was in the beginning stage of my business, one of my first design projects was in a high-end luxury home. While we focused mostly on fresh paint, furnishings, and overall décor, it was also my responsibility to design and manage the construction of a wet bar for the games room that was worth more than double what my own kitchen cost. The clients had an upcoming event that the bar needed to be ready for, which meant that we were now looking at a rush job. From concept to execution, the project was completed in a matter of weeks. I had never completed a project of this caliber in such a short period of time – it was stressful, it was challenging, and it was absolutely exhilarating! Since this was my first big project, I was a little out of my realm and feeling not as prepared as I could have been. I spent a TON of time trying to figure out each next step, trying desperately to ensure that nothing was overlooked, under-measured, or forgotten. I felt like I was stumbling through it, and in the end, I learned a very valuable lesson about having detailed processes for future projects. Lesson learned! In the end, the bar looked fabulous, I had some very happy clients, a great project for my portfolio, and the confidence to tackle anything and everything.

Despite this confidence, I found the sales aspect of managing my own business challenging. I had always been great at sales. Heck, I was a vegetarian working at a steakhouse when I started my business, and I sold more dinner features than anyone else in the restaurant! But finding the methodology for selling myself, and my services, was different. No matter how hard I seemed to work at it, the phone just wasn't ringing the way that I thought that it should be. So I took a step back from my business and refocused. I spent some time revising my business plan, rebranding my company, and relaunching the business with a new perspective and direction. I had made two critical mistakes. The first was that I didn't fully understand that while the design and home staging aspects of my business crossed over, and I would often find myself working with the same clients on both sides, the marketing for each was different. This was due in large part to how the processes for each differed.

The next mistake was directly related to the first: I didn't understand who my ideal clients were. I had worked in a number of luxury homes, and thought that perhaps this was the niche market that I wanted to stay in, but I also found that I enjoyed the challenge of working with clients that were on a budget. Once I was able to embrace these varying loves, I was able to sit down and create an avatar of my ideal client. While I didn't need to serve everyone, I was able to identify specific characteristics that I was looking for in my clients that would cross over various income levels.

I love helping my clients by providing small bits of advice with huge impacts. When I am working in a home that is being listed for sale, the most common and most effective alteration that I make to the home is in the furniture arrangement. While most homeowners tend to place their furniture in locations that are convenient for living, this layout may not represent the most optimal flow for selling. After showing my home staging clients the new furniture arrangement, they almost always react, "Oh my goodness, why didn't I think of this sooner?" Of course, my response is that they didn't have me! Now those same clients that I worked with for staging are now calling me after their home has sold to ask me if I can assist them in their new home. They've already witnessed the magic of what I can do. One of a home stager's greatest gifts is their ability to work with a homeowner's own items to maximize the look of their space. Often called "staging for living," the service of *redesign* utilizes the techniques of home staging, but applies them for living, not selling, to create a cohesive design.

The first thing that you need to know about home staging is that it's a *marketing technique* for homes that are listed for sale. This means that home staging operates in the real estate industry just as much, if not more than, in the design industry. More and more we are seeing these two industries collide, as home staging incorporates more on-trend design elements than ever, and designers have discovered that home staging is a fantastic complement to an already fabulous career.

The redesign industry, which emerged from home staging, has made decorating and redesign services much more accessible to all homeowners. There was a time when interior design was perceived to be reserved for the elite. The home staging approach provides a step-by-step service that allows homeowners to make decisions along the way about how much, or how little, they wish to spend, depending on their desired outcome. It starts with a consultation for a reasonable fee. This consultation provides easy-to-implement tips and a do-it-yourself plan of action. Following the consultation, the homeowner may choose to simply take the advice and put it into action themselves, or to hire the home staging company to provide an additional level of service, such as selecting finishes for some updates or declutter. Alternately, the client may select full-service home staging, which includes the rental of and installation of select furnishings, accessories, artwork, and more to complete the look. This "a la carte" style of providing services can often help to accommodate a variety of budgets. Home staging and redesign have helped to take away some of the perceived intimidation of the interior design industry. While redesign is not intended to replace interior design services, it has opened up a new market. We live in an age of specialization with a "hire a pro" type of attitude, as opposed to the popular Do-It-Yourself phase of years past. This systematic process provides home stagers and designers a foot in the door with a simple consultation and allows them the opportunity to build on that with additional layers of service.

Working in someone's home is a very personal experience, and it is truly a privilege to be invited into their home and into their lives. As designers, we delve deep into the various aspects of our clients' lives—this is how we create our best concepts, both in terms of style, and function. We become almost a part of the family; this is especially true when you are working with clients that you actually like! When you create a positive experience, you build a trust that continues to develop and grow over time. Think about your relationship with your hairstylist or your mechanic – it's important that you trust this person, and therefore when you find the right fit, you are highly likely to remain loyal, and keep coming back time and again! In fact, I am so loyal to my hairstylists that I have had very few over the course of my life, and I have followed them from location to location, regardless of how far I have had to drive to get to them. Not only that, but I have helped them to grow their business through word-of-mouth referrals and shout-outs on social media. I even carry their business cards in my wallet to easily share when someone inquires about whom I trust with my hair (usually randomly while waiting in line at the grocery store). I'm a walking billboard for my hairstylist, and I am thrilled to share my love of this gem with anyone that I meet. When we find a relationship that benefits us, and that is well worth the investment of both time and money, we want to tell everyone—after all, commodities like these work best when shared. If they go out of business, where will that leave you?

The relationship between a designer and their clients is an intimate one and can be an ever-lasting bond – this bond means that your clients are likely to call you back each time that they have a new project that they are working on. Repeat business is one of THE best types of business! These clients already understand the process, they already regard your work and believe in your vision, they understand your rates, and trust in your value and your worth. We love it when our clients are loyal and keep coming back for more. I have some clients that I have worked with through several renovation projects, AND I have helped them to sell their home as well when the time came to move into the next phase of their life, whatever that was. Sometimes the design aspect comes first; sometimes it's the home staging service that comes first. Either way, these clients don't make a single decision on their home without first consulting with me. I had a couple who once hired me to decorate their living room. This project then turned into a full basement renovation with wet bar, then a small kitchen facelift. It came to point that they would call me when they needed to purchase new flooring vents, just to get my approval on them. I went on to later help them to prepare their home for sale-which they found especially amusing as I removed most of the custom decorating elements I had previously installed in favor of more neutral options-and of course, I assisted them again in their new home. They love to entertain, and they never miss an opportunity to inform their friends of their fantastic designer (and home stager) that has been an integral influence for their last two homes. This kind of loyalty cannot be bought. It's earned, and it is invaluable.

Your clients already trust you, and they want you to help them with every home décor and design decision, including preparing their home for sale. As mentioned earlier, while home staging and design concepts overlap in numerous ways, there are just as many fundamental differences between the two. Before venturing into the unknown unprepared, it is important to fully understand what these are in order to properly and effectively address each one. If you work in interior design, you may have noticed that a number of industry professionals have added home staging to their list of services in the last few years. Home staging can be a great complementary service to a creative-based service portfolio, but how do you know if it's right for you? What some may love about home staging, others might see as a deal-breaker and a reason to stick strictly with design.

Home staging is an effective sales technique that integrates decorating with marketing and creates an experience for buyers. It's about more than just furnishing a home – it's about selling a lifestyle. How do we do this? By creating a move-in ready home for buyers, which is no small feat. Home stagers do this by clearly identifying and showcasing the home's greatest features. Home staging focuses on the buyers, what they're looking for, what they see when they preview a home, and what perceptions they will create. Creating the best home staging design plan for a space is about understanding the demographics of the neighbourhood, city, and style of home that you are working in. It is a home stager's responsibility to minimize or eliminate all possible distractions that could take the potential buyer's focus away from the home's selling features.

I have come to know a number of home stagers over the years who started out in the field of design, only to realize that their true passion was for home staging. In fact, one of my home staging team members received her diploma in Interior Design, but she found that the hands-on application and instant gratification that home staging provided was more her speed. This is not to say that you need to choose one over the other, but you might find that it will fulfill something that's been missing for you.

There are a number of benefits to adding home staging to your existing design business:

- Expand your service market reach
- Build long-term relationships with homeowners
- Strengthen relationships with suppliers by offering additional sales opportunities
- Increase your revenue stream
- Manage peaks and valleys of the business
- Tap into a large network of potential new business by working with real estate agents
- Keep your designs fresh and fluid with an ever-changing market and industry, and the exposure to a greater number of homes
- Improve cash flow – home staging services are usually paid in full up front, and rental renewals can generate a passive recurring revenue (more on this later)
- Experience the thrill of immediate and quick results
- Every day is a new adventure!

These are just a few of my favorite reasons to explore home staging. That said, don't be misled – while these two industries overlap and share a number of similar traits, there are just as many fundamental differences. Let's start with where we differ. As an interior decorator or interior designer, you work with a client's overall style to create a design plan that reflects their needs. You review their likes and their dislikes, as well as their functional needs for everyday living. As a home stager, you work with the home's overall style to create your staging plan, based on the neighbourhood, house characteristics, and target buyer demographics. Your aim is to appeal to the largest variety of buyers possible, so you avoid making overly specific and personal design choices, especially in terms of the hard finishes. Ultimately the client's personal likes and dislikes will not factor into the final plan (for many home staging professionals, this can be the best part of home staging). Your ultimate goal is to sell the house, and in order to achieve this, you need to *merchandise* the home to effectively market it. While function should always play a role, some standard comfort of living is often sacrificed in order to create the best overall look and feel.

In the world of interior decorating and interior design, you are often creating and designing the focal elements of a room. This may include hard elements such as a unique flooring choice or light fixture. It might include statement furnishings, or an eye-catching one-of-a-kind custom art piece. In the world of home staging, your goal is to neutralize the space, and eliminate any distractions that could take the focus away from the appealing selling features of the house. For this reason, statement pieces are often avoided in favor of more neutral selections. While in design, more is generally better, in home staging, less is more. It's the Goldilocks scenario—not too much, not too little, but just right. When I'm designing a space for living, I love to incorporate personal elements into the overall design concept to create a comfortable home for the owners, such as a family name custom art piece, or a family heirloom given a new life and purpose. In home staging, personal items are removed in order to eliminate this potential distraction. Buyers need to envision themselves in the home, and an overly personalized space can lose its desired effect.

One of the most appealing aspects of home staging as a business is instant gratification. While design projects can often take several months to complete, most home staging projects are completed in less than a month from consult to completion, and in some cases they can be completed in a matter of a few days or even hours! Be warned, though—the gratification of these instant results can be addicting. This quick turnaround is achievable because of the home staging system. While each house is unique, the overall system from start to finish for home staging is fairly consistent, and there is a formula that can be followed. In design, with so many variables and factors available to be changed, renovated, and reconfigured, the design concepts alone can take months to sort out before finally breaking ground and putting the ideas into action. In home staging, there is a very clear starting point, and an even clearer conclusion to the project.

This systematic approach to home staging and established industry standards can make pricing home staging services fairly straightforward. While each home staging company will apply a different technique for creating their prices, there are set formulas your home staging certification course will outline, taking much of the guesswork out of this element. Of course, in a number of areas, home staging and interior design will overlap. In fact, this is where your formal design training will really help you to shine in the field of home staging and will set you up for success.

As in all room designs, proper furniture placement is essential to the execution of a successful staging plan. Not only will standard placement rules apply as they would in design, but the traffic flow in a home is especially important to the overall sell-ability. Buyers can be easily turned off or distracted by out-of-place furnishings. Just as room flow can affect the comfort of a room for living, improper flow in a home for sale can easily turn off buyers without their even realizing it! A disruption in their path as they move through the home can affect buyers on a subconscious level and prevent them from placing an offer on the property.

In home staging, your furniture placement is often creating a blueprint of sorts for buyers, showcasing the ideal positioning of the furnishings in each room. Each room should be clearly defined, and multi-purpose rooms (often the backbone of design plans, especially in small spaces, in order to help to maximize a client's space) are strongly discouraged in home staging, often leading buyers to believe that the home may not have enough space for their daily needs. A well-thought-out home staging plan will create a warm, welcoming space.

Current home trends are used in moderation in home staging and should only be applied through accessory decor. Permanent elements and fixtures, such as flooring or backsplashes, should remain neutral and should be selected in classic and timeless styles. Remember that in home staging, our goal is to direct potential buyers' focus towards the features of the home; a home's staging should not overshadow the home's built-in elements.

Just as in design, it is your responsibility to provide your clients with all the recommendations that you feel that they could benefit from, and it is also your responsibility to guide them toward the highest-priority items versus those that may have less impact. The highest-priority items in home staging will be those items that will provide the greatest return on their investment in the sale of their home, as well as those items that are likely to be a deal-breaker for potential buyers if not addressed. This is an important area that a formal training program will explore further and help you to identify.

You will also have a budget to work with, just as you do with your design clients. However, in the case of selling a home, there is often less perceived flexibility in the budget because clients will not have the opportunity to appreciate the updates once their home is sold. At times, you may need to address the value of increasing the budget in order to help clients see the big picture. In some cases, you may not actually have a budget at all. Your goal may simply be to do the best that you can with what you have to work with through your home staging consultation service. While some home stagers find this restraint to be challenging, I have found it to be a rewarding aspect. Not all reasons to sell a home are happy ones. While it can be fun to help your clients to move on to an exciting new chapter in their lives, sometimes the part that you play in helping to sell a client's home is to help them close a chapter they would sooner forget. From divorce, to death, to bankruptcy, home stagers see it all, and knowing that you have helped someone to move on from a difficult time in their lives can provide a greater satisfaction than any amount of money can provide.

As often happens in business, despite your best efforts and planning, things sometimes go wrong. Ensuring that you have a clear understanding of your standard operating procedures (SOPs) and clearly outlined home staging contracts for your staging projects will help to minimize these occasions and manage them when they arise. Here are just a few examples of some situations that can arise:

- A property is not ready for staging on the day of install (i.e., renovations are still being completed or homeowners' items have not moved out).
- Home staging inventory may be damaged, or stolen, from a staged property.
- Staging with pets and kids—need I say more?
- Staging in any weather—including snow storms, rain storms, wind storms, and more—can create challenging situations and unexpected delays.
- Not every client actually wants to hear what you have to say—often, you have been hired by the real estate agent, not the homeowner, and the homeowner may be reluctant to heed your professional advice.
- The real estate agent may not agree with advice that you have provided to their client. If the real estate agent has hired you (for at least the initial consultation), you will need to ensure that you maintain a balance of keeping ALL of your clients happy – that means ensuring that the homeowners' needs are met, while also being a supportive part of the home-selling team and the real estate agent who hired you.
- Overdue or late payments—it might interest you to know that the standard payment terms for home staging projects is to have it paid in full PRIOR to staging! While design can be very subjective, and is often billed in phases throughout the project, home staging, given its quick turn-around, is billed and collected quickly.
- Clients often have a different idea of "clean." It may be your responsibility to identify where they have missed the mark.
- A variety of cultures and customs can pose challenges when it comes to selling a home
- Sometimes, the house doesn't sell! You need to manage your clients' expectations and understanding of the role that you play in the home-selling process.

While many home stylists will cross over both industries, and enjoy the challenges that each brings, others prefer to work in their creative niche and comfort zone. In a recent poll of home stagers, I identified that 77 percent of those surveyed offer both home staging and design services, and 15 percent of them begin in the field of design! The diversity of offering both services can help to keep you on top of your game in each. Home staging is a great complementary service for design professionals, putting their creative skills to work within a setting that offers quick turn-around and outcome. Let's face it: eventually your design clients will sell their house, and that will allow you to easily turn these same clients into home staging clients.

Misconceptions abound about what home staging is and what it isn't. When home staging was first introduced, it was meant as a way to incorporate some "lifestyle" aspects to a home and set a stage for living. While some think of home staging as mostly decluttering and pillow fluffing, others think of it as a dramatic transformation, replacing all furnishings/accessories with new staged items. Home staging can be all of these things and more. The process of home staging is about addressing all areas of improvement for a home in order to create the greatest appeal for home buyers. In the initial consultation, home stagers will address all updates, repairs, furniture rearrangements, and styling additions to a home that will help to create a move-in ready home that buyers are not only interested in buying but are willing to pay more money for! The days of purchasing a home only to fix it up to your liking are becoming a thing of the past. While many homeowners will eventually make some improvements to the home, big and small, they want to know that they can move in immediately and have the ability to comfortably entertain. My extensive experience in home renovations has helped me to better understand the various expenses associated with any updates or repairs and allow me to better identify the most cost-effective solutions for my clients.

According to the 2017 Profile of Buyers and Sellers by the National Association of Realtors®:

- 42 percent of buyers began the home buying process by looking online at properties for sale (before contacting a real estate agent)
- Buyers typically searched for 10 weeks and looked at a median of 10 homes
- 36 percent of buyers who purchased new homes were looking to avoid renovations and problems with plumbing or electricity

Due to the rising price of homeownership, today's homebuyers are purchasing at the top of their purchasing power and are therefore much more inclined to purchase a home that has addressed any necessary updates and renovations. They want the home to be move-in ready and allow them to entertain immediately. While they may choose to do some renovations and updates at a later date, they want a home that they can enjoy now.

With millennials as the largest share of home buyers in 2018 at 36 percent (according to the 2018 Home Buyer and Seller Generational Trends Report by the National Association of Realtors®), we will see an even greater shift towards move-in ready homes as even younger buyers enter the homebuyer's market. This is a generation that has only known a digital world and have a strong desire for convenience and instant reward.

As mentioned earlier, there is a clear formula and systematic approach to home staging. You will usually start with a consultation. Whereas in design, the consultation is usually viewed as a starting point, in home staging, this could be the only service that the client hires you for. This consultation will provide a comprehensive do-it-yourself list of tasks for the homeowner to complete. The fee for this can vary by location, but it is always a billed service. The homeowner(s) can then choose to hire you to manage and complete the list that you have provided them with, or they can tackle the tasks themselves. Here's a snapshot of what this looks like:

1. Consultation with report of recommendations.
2. Provide bid/proposal for additional services—if accepted, send contract and invoice.
3. Recommendations from the consultation are implemented (either by you as the home staging company, or by the client, or a combination of both).
4. House is cleaned—and I mean white glove clean. It is highly recommended that the homeowners enlist professional help with this aspect. This is always done prior to staging.
5. Home stager returns to the house with the home staging items required (if the client accepted the bid).
6. Professional photos are taken—these may be a part of your service package as the home stager or may be arranged by the real estate agent.

    Note: if you wish to have photos for your portfolio, you will need to arrange for these. Photographers often charge for additional rights to using their photos, so you may not be able to share the agent's photos legally. Also, the photos taken for selling the property may not showcase your work as well as they could.
7. The listing hits the market! This means that it is listed on the MLS (Multiple Listings Service), and private showings or open houses are scheduled.
8. Your job as a home stager is not complete until the house has sold, but if the home has been staged with home staging items, you will need to successfully de-stage the property before you can close the file.

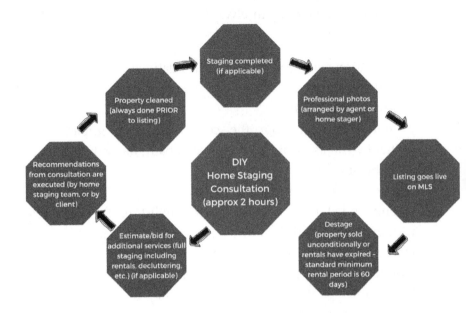

You may choose to specialize in only vacant or only owner-occupied home staging projects, or you may opt to offer both services. You can choose the model that best fits with your current business structure, your availability, and your overall needs. There are successful business models of every variety, and any of these models can be profitable if executed correctly. I recommend deciding which direction you wish to go in after you have completed your home staging training and have had some experience working in the field. The direction you choose will be dependent on a number of factors, including whether or not you wish to invest in home staging inventory and the storage and transportation that this will entail, your ability to work with an established look/style, your preference to work with a blank slate, your desire to work in a multitude of homes, your ability to work with a home staging team of professionals, and your ability to execute large scale projects in a short timeframe.

By now, you may be thinking seriously about adding home staging to your interior design business. Education never ends, at least for great designers. Home staging is a great way to round out your knowledge, and to continue to grow as a designer and establish yourself as a home expert.

How ready are you to become a home stager? Take the quiz!

Score 1 point for each "yes" answer:

1. Do you have peaks and valleys in your business?
2. Do you enjoy new adventures each day?
3. Do you adjust well to an ever-changing schedule?
4. Are you solutions-focused?
5. Are you good at thinking on your feet?
6. Do you enjoy problem solving?
7. Are you willing to work long hours when necessary to achieve quick results?
8. Do you build long-lasting and ongoing relationships with your clients?
9. Are you organized?
10. Do you have a thick skin?
11. Are you physically fit (or interested in being more active each day)?
12. Do you have strong renovation knowledge?
13. Do you enjoy shopping?
14. Do you have strong wholesale relationships with quality vendors already on your speed dial?
15. Do you work well with different personality types?
16. Can you manage objections and resistance from clients who may fear change?
17. Do you understand the return on investment of large and small home renovations?
18. Are you interested in the real estate market?
19. Are you able to express your ideas and vision verbally?
20. Do you have the flexibility to work on an accelerated time frame?

Did you score ten points or higher on this quiz? If so, you're ready to kick off your home staging adventures! To learn more about what your future in home staging holds, and how to get started, book a personalized call with me at: www.StyledListedSold.com/PowerFridayStaging.

Does this business model interest you after learning about the differences between home staging and interior design?

Keep in mind that, beyond the question of if you would enjoy home staging, there is the matter of learning the process for home staging. As Shauna Lynn explained, they are not the same business. They aren't even in the same industry, technically. The timelines are different, the services are different, and the fee structures are different. Just as you cannot apply the same design principles to home staging, you cannot apply the same business systems for interior design to home staging. They may be related but they are not the same. To be successful, keep this in mind.

I do love two aspects of combining your interior design practice with home staging services. If you can do both well, and if you set up finite systems for each model, I love how the home staging clients have the potential to turn into interior design clients, and vice versa. You can build a relationship, earn their trust by doing terrific work on one side, and educate them on the need for the other service. Shauna Lynn described the client who asked her to design their home for living, and, when it came time to sell, hired her to design it for selling. She had to check her own ego at the door and focus on the new objective: to sell the house. She explained how she removed many of the custom details she herself had specified. The new goal was for the décor to appeal to many, not to her or to her existing clients. That story contains such a wonderful lesson and observation.

The other aspect I love is the argument for redesign for living as a valuable ladder of service. Not every client wants or can afford full-service design. This is an underserved niche. With so many designers truly only interested in providing full-service design, it leaves the market wide open to attract all the homeowners who simply want their home to just look put together. *You, as a designer, take for granted the ability to walk in a room and know things are not properly placed. The art is too high, the sofa is in the wrong place, and the lighting is all wrong. Homeowners who will never in their entire lives hire a full-service designer would still like their home to look and feel right. You come in, suggest some new accessories, new paint colors and a few other easy changes and, voila, it's night and day.*

I know many designers run from this market segment in search of full-service clients. That is their right. As a business owner, you design the business you want to have, as long as you make money doing it. Others make the wrong assumption that redesign is easy. The truth is, it is often more difficult, because you are constrained by the existing possessions. Working around the husband's prized reclining chair is a real thing. However, meeting the challenge, transforming a room using your client's limited resources, your creativity, and your talented eye can be immensely rewarding. Beware! Scope creep, favorite chairs, and resistance to change are all real obstacles to this design model. However, if you love to make lemons out of lemonade, redesign can be rewarding and profitable.

The big takeaway is that if you decide to add home staging to your business model, learn the proper project systems, pricing structures, and design principles to ensure your success.

- LN

About the Author

Shauna Lynn Simon is an award-winning home staging industry expert and business strategist committed to guiding aspiring entrepreneurs to achieve success in their business. After building a thriving home staging and design business, she founded Styled, Listed, and Sold (SLS) Academy, a comprehensive and systematic program providing core and continuing education training for home staging professionals.

Shauna Lynn has appeared on LuAnn's podcast three times, on episodes 76, 84, and 102:

https://luannnigara.com/76-shauna-lynn-simon-home-staging-is-not-interior-design-and-heres-why/

https://luannnigara.com/84-shauna-lynn-simon-how-to-host-a-successful-interior-design-consumer-event-in-your-community/

https://luannnigara.com/102-power-talk-friday-shauna-lynn-simon-part-2-how-to-host-a-successful-consumer-event-for-your-community/

CHAPTER 11

Kae Whitaker

I am often asked by designers I coach, "Should I hire someone to do my digital marketing and my social media marketing?" I always answer, "Yes and no."

If you have a mature business, like mine, Window Works, and if you have the ability to hire an awesome company to execute your digital marketing and social media strategies, then please look into it. If you do not, you may not want to do this too soon.

Why is it okay for me?

Because both at Window Works and at my personal platform I know what we do, who we do it for, how we do it, and who I want to attract in the doing of it. Without knowing these things, you cannot put it in the hands of someone else. It hardly stands a chance of representing you, your ideals, and your vision. If it doesn't represent you and your company in a genuine and identifiable way, it cannot work effectively to attract the right client to you.

Consider this: if someone asked you to design their home, top to bottom, you'd ask dozens of questions about lifestyle, aesthetics, budget, color preferences, and so on. Now imagine every single answer was, "I don't know. You're the designer, you tell me."

Don't rush by this! Sit and truly imagine working on a project with a client who had no clue at all about style, design, furniture, or lighting, and also had no insight as to their own personal design preferences. How could you design their home? Where would you start?

Somehow, we expect a marketing firm to be successful when we are as unprepared as the client above. A professional marketing firm will do the same as you do when preparing for a new project. They will ask you all the pertinent questions about your company, about your super power, about your ideal client, about your persona, your image, your genuine self, and how you want to be seen. Do you have the answers? Or will you say, "You're the expert; you figure it out."

To be clear, I know you could design a home without the client's personal profile, just as marketing firms can design a marketing plan without your personal profile. The question is, how successful will either of these outcomes be under these conditions?

It makes perfect sense now, doesn't it?

You must know certain things about yourself and your business and you must be able to express them before you can expect any consultant to do their job effectively. Whether it is designing a home or designing a marketing campaign, the client has to be an active, knowledgeable partner in the process and to do that, they have to know their vision, their ideals and their goal.

I invited Kae to write this chapter because she shares a very clear description of both the client journey and the companion description for the email sequence that accompanies the client journey. The understanding of these two concepts are the foundation for outlining your digital marketing plan. As you read her chapter, try to identify which step in the journey each of your current clients and prospective clients are currently occupying, thinking about the needs they have in each step. Remember, all lead generation, digital or otherwise, starts with a clear understanding of your client's point of view of their needs.

- LN

Elevate Your Email Marketing: Understanding the Client Journey
By Kae Whitaker

When it comes to email marketing, most think that it's an extension of your online marketing. The reality is that, if implemented correctly, email marketing is a valuable tool that can be initiated both online and offline. As a designer, so many opportunities to build your email lists can be found in trade shows, markets, industry events, and, of course, social media, that it's important that you understand how to set up a system that will not only support your online goals but also transfer to those many activities that you conduct offline as well.

With that said, it's important as a designer to understand the right and wrong ways to use email marketing and how to effectively implement a strategy into your business that will help you accomplish your revenue goals from your efforts both online and offline.

Just for a moment, why don't we discuss what email marketing is and how it can help you build your design business, sometimes even on autopilot. That's the sweetest part of this all! Let's begin.

What is email marketing?

Email marketing is the process of using email as a means of building a relationship with a prospect to move them through one step of the customer journey to the next with your company.

Contrary to popular belief, it's not just a selling tool; its primary goal is to keep your customers engaged in a process with you that will eventually lead to sales, which we call the customer journey.

The customer journey serves as a gauge for you, as the designer, to know exactly where your prospects are relating to their relationship with you. A solid understanding of the customer journey helps you to know when it's time to make the right offer to move them from just being prospects into actual paying clients.

Email marketing is the tool that we use within this customer journey that helps us to facilitate this relationship, which is why it's so important that you understand the customer journey and how to plug email marketing into it to move your prospects into customers.

For the next few minutes, let's spend some time getting acquainted with the customer journey. Then we'll look at how to plug email marketing into this journey to make it work.

What is the Customer Journey?

The customer journey is an eight-step relationship process that your prospects go through with your business. Whether you have been aware of this journey or not, at some point, each of your prospects have taken a step in this journey with you, which has led them to become a customer.

For some of us, we've missed a few steps, which is what has caused us not to see the success that we desire from our efforts and, more specifically, our email efforts; my goal for you is to teach you this process so you can better understand where your prospects are and know which email to send to help you move them into the next part of the journey with you.

The Eight Steps along the Customer Journey

There are eight steps to this customer journey that I want to outline in this section. Within each of these eight steps, an appropriate email or communication will need to be sent to effectively move your prospects into the next step of the journey with you.

We'll outline the eight steps first, then we'll go back to understand where email marketing comes in, and which type of email should be sent in each part of the journey to be effective.

Once you've completed the chapter, you'll also find a link at the end of the chapter that will provide a free workbook to download that will help you to map out your journey, as well as know which emails you should send so you can get active online.

Step 1: Awareness. This may seem clear, but this is where your prospects first become acquainted with who you are and what your business stands for. While this seems like a logical first step, you'd be surprised to know just how many businesses forget that there needs to be a proper introduction to their business, and it needs to be an amazing one to gain the interest of your prospects. The content that you create at this stage of the journey is referred to as "top of funnel" content, which is where the journey begins.

Think first impression here.

Everything you create should be created with the idea that you are trying to impress someone who has never encountered you before. If you do that, you'll be surprised by how many more people you can get to move into the next step of the journey, which is Engagement.

As a designer, some of your prospects may become aware of your business through trade shows, social media, referrals, and the like, so it's important that you are always on top of your game here, as you never know where you'll run into your next potential client.

Make sense?

Step 2: Engagement. This is the part of the journey where your prospects will start to take the next step in the relationship with you and send signals that they are interested in what you have to offer. In this step of the journey, they may start to follow you online, they may visit your website and read one of your articles, or they may begin to watch some of your videos online. This is where they begin to show interest in your brand. Email hasn't come into the picture yet, but if you do a good job of engaging your prospects through rich content, then you'll be glad to know that at the next step of the journey you'll begin to be able to implement some email strategies that can work on autopilot for you for the next few steps of the journey that will lead to sales for your company.

Step 3: Subscription. This is where the rubber meets the road. In this step of the journey, your prospects have agreed that they find value in the relationship that you all have started to build. They are now ready to take your relationship a step further.

If you liken this process to a romantic relationship, this is where the interested party asks for those digits and you, as the candidate of their choice, oblige. We're at a pivotal point in the relationship now, because the prospect has agreed to move from a public, more general, relationship with you, into a deeper, more intimate conversation, which now takes place in their email inbox.

This is huge. When you reach this point with a prospect, you should rejoice, because an email address these days is just like the exchange of a phone number. If you're effective in your email strategy and take special care of your prospect's needs, from this point forward you could soon be seeing the monetary gains from your efforts, which I'm sure is where we'd all like to end up.

We'll talk a little later in the chapter about what types of emails should be used in this step of the journey to make this a relationship worth keeping for your prospects.

Step 4: Conversion. In this step of the journey you've earned the right to ask your prospect to do something for you now.

The previous three steps have represented a one-way relationship where you've been in hot pursuit, but if you handle them with care in the subscription step of the journey, you can safely use your email marketing to then ask them to convert from just being a subscriber on your list into taking the first steps to becoming a customer.

Now something to note in this step is that conversion is not always attached to a dollar amount the first time a prospect goes through this journey with you.

As a designer, your conversion could possibly be the prospective client scheduling a call with you to discuss the needs of their upcoming project.

It's important to understand this principle, because in the next step of the journey is where you'll start to see some revenue come into your account. The emails that you send at this stage of the journey are going to help you to make this process happen a lot smoother for you and your new client.

Step 5: Excitement. In the excitement stage of the journey, it's important to note that when you move your prospects from engagement to conversion, you've got to deliver something they can get excited about that makes them want to purchase.

As a designer, you may deliver an incredible presentation on how you can handle the intricacies of your prospects' project. If they can see the light at the end of the tunnel, you've successfully got them excited about what you offer. Yes, there is a particular email that you send in this stage of the journey that will get them to the next step, and believe it or not, it's as easy as 1, 2, 3.

We'll outline what that email is in just a few minutes here.

Step 6: Ascension. At this step of the journey your prospects are now becoming customers! There is an official exchange of revenue and you have officially gained a new client. Hooray!

Your hard work has paid off and now we just need to deliver on what we've promised in the excitement stage of the journey.

Your emails here will become few and further between as you'll be taking your prospect physically by the hand, but you'll be glad to know that all the work that you put into getting them to this point through your email marketing has paid off and has provided the proper return on investment of time!

Step 7: Advocacy. In the advocacy part of the journey, you'll begin to ask your customers now to tell someone else about their experience. This may be through asking for testimonials, reviews, or the like. It's in this stage where you've delivered on your promise, given results, and have earned the right to turn your now client into a brand advocate for your business.

This is the stage where most designers fall off, fail to use their emails to their advantage, and miss, quite frankly, a very easy opportunity to move a client into the next step of the journey and make gaining another client just like them that much easier.

If at this point you have a happy client, you should not overlook this portion of the journey. A specific email can be sent out at this point to make this process easier for you and your client.

Step 8: Promotion. When you've done your job and delivered on what you promised, it's very easy to turn your clients into active promoters of your business.

Email marketing in this stage of the journey is very important because this is the moment that you'll begin to give specific instructions on what's next for you and your client.

I want you to remember something.

Just because you've finished rendering a service for your client at this point, doesn't mean that the journey is over just yet. Until your client becomes an active promoter of your business, you still have work to do. At this point if they are happy, they'll be more than happy to participate in the process with you.

Your emails at this point are guaranteed to be opened and are a lot easier to get your clients to act.

With that, in the next section of this chapter, we're going to go back through this customer journey and highlight which emails you should send at each stage of the journey.

I'll tell you how many emails of each kind will be appropriate. Believe it or not, this is a very simple task to complete and will make moving your prospects along the journey with you much easier than you think.

Let's move on.

Sending the Right Emails at the Right Time

Now that you understand the journey that your prospects are taking with you, let's go back and figure out just what type of emails you should be sending at each stage of the journey and how many of those emails should do the trick.

Don't forget at the end of the chapter there's a link to a free workbook that will help you through this process as well, this might be a good time to skip ahead and go download the workbook then come back to complete this process.

Step 1: Becoming Aware. Congratulations! At this point you don't have a lot of work to do, as the prospect is just getting acquainted with you and you don't have their email address just yet. Even though you aren't sending them emails directly, I want you to think about something right here.

If you have an email list, it's likely that you are sending some form of communication out to your list at least once or twice a month. This might look like a newsletter or an update about the company. If it's nicely prepared, your brand advocates are likely sharing it with their friends.

While this may seem redundant to include in a newsletter, I want you to make sure that at the end of each of your newsletters, you inject a little call to action for a reader who may have been on the receiving end of your newsletter via a friend forwarding it to them.

This call to action may read something like the following:

"Did you receive this email from a friend, and do you want to become a part of our community? You can do so by subscribing to our tribe. You will receive these emails directly into your inbox from us weekly (or whatever your timing may be). Join us here—(include the link to subscribe)."

By doing this, you've captured a new audience through your already engaged audience.

Step 2: Engagement. Just as in the first step, even though you don't have your prospect's email yet, I would be sure to follow the instructions that I've included about adding that appendix to your email newsletter, so you can actively engage the readers of your newsletters who may not be subscribers yet.

If you use the proper email management system, you can see when your emails are being forwarded. When you see this practice happening often, you'll want to maximize the audience who are not yet on your list.

Step 3: Subscription. This is where email starts to play a part in moving your customer through this journey.

At the subscription stage, your prospect has now trusted you with their email, so you have to make an amazing first impression here.

In this step, two emails are necessary to move your customers along the next part of the journey with you. They are the confirmation email and the delivery email.

Let's look at each one to see how it works.

The confirmation email: this email serves as a confirmation for you, as the business owner, to ensure that you have the proper email address on file. When a prospect subscribes to your offer, you want to make sure that the email address is spelled correctly and that they have indeed asked for what you are getting ready to send.

The great news about this email is that it is automatically sent through your email service provider, so you don't have to create it. You'll just want to indicate that you want your prospect to have to do what's called "double opt-in" and your email provider will handle the rest for you.

Once your prospect has confirmed their email address, you'll want to send them what they asked for, which is what I call the delivery email.

Let's look at what the delivery email should accomplish. The delivery email should accomplish two things. 1) It should deliver what you prospect asked for, right? 2) It should also set the tone for what the prospect can expect from you in the future through your emails.

You should have something created to offer to your prospects for no cost to get them to subscribe to your email list. This would be something like an eBook, checklist, video, or a document that outlines something special in your industry which your prospect has questions about that you can answer quickly.

For a designer it might be latest trends for the season, how to do something like pick a paint color for the bedroom, and so on. The possibilities are endless.

If you're not sure how to create what I like to call a "freemium," that's another conversation for another day, but the main goal of this delivery email is to send it to them.

Remember that your emails are moving your prospects through a journey with you, so you want to pay special attention to making sure you're using each one of your emails to let the prospect know what's next in this journey. This way, they aren't blindsided when they receive another email from you.

This delivery email should explain to them that they'll be receiving more emails from you soon and what they can expect from these emails.

I call these future emails an "indoctrination" campaign. This campaign is what we'll use in the next step to help your prospects Convert.

Which is the next step of your customer journey, let's look at how that works.

Step 4: Conversion. The conversion stage of the journey is for indoctrinating prospects into who you are and how you work. This is the time where you'll use your past experiences and a little bit of information to move your prospects from mere email subscribers into actual potential customers.

Let's look at a few emails that should be included in your indoctrination campaign.

The Indoctrination Campaign: in this series of emails you may send several, maybe five to seven, emails over the course of a couple of weeks. The goal of these emails should be to accomplish the following:

1. Introduce your company and the brains behind the operation.
2. Share content that you may have created on your blog that others have enjoyed.
3. Share testimonials from other customers.
4. Provide examples of your work.
5. Most importantly, ask them to book some time with you to discuss their needs.

This point in the journey is probably the most intricate and the one that you'll spend the most time on. Sharing the right content and more importantly asking your prospect to convert in your emails is what's going to keep them moving through the journey.

Don't be afraid to ask in your emails. If you don't ask, they won't know what's expected of them and they won't do anything.

In your email relationship, you're the driver of the relationship. You're in control. If you understand the journey that you're trying to take them on, sharing the right content becomes easier. Based on their behavior, you'll know when to ask them to move forward.

Step 5: Excitement. At this point, your prospects have converted into leads for your business. They've agreed to meet with you, which is amazing. One email can be sent in this stage of the journey that will make that meeting so much easier and ensure that your lead is prepared for your time together.

It's the "Here's what you should expect" or "Do this to be ready" email. In short, it's another confirmation email. However, in this email, the goals are different than when your lead initially subscribed to your list. Let's look at what the confirmation email at this part of the journey should include.

The Meeting Confirmation Email. At this point your prospects have officially become leads and they should be excited about what they are getting into. To keep this excitement and make your time together more productive, you can have your leads do a few things in this confirmation email to set up your meeting. Things I would suggest including in your email are:

1) Meeting expectations: Should they bring anything? How long will it take? Where will it take place?

2) Pre-meeting questionnaires, if applicable: Most designers want to know a few things about the project to be prepared. This is a perfect time to ask them to complete the questionnaire. It saves time in the meeting and gives you a general idea of their needs before you meet.

Sending this email further engages your now-lead into your process. It ensures that they show up for your scheduled time together, and it gives them something further to look forward to.

They are now an active part of this process. The more active they are, the higher your conversion rates will be, because they almost feel as though they are leading the relationship and have some skin in the game.

If you haven't noticed, not once have we talked about your newsletters yet, because those aren't important just yet.

Right now, we are actively turning subscribers into buyers. Have you gotten excited yet?

Step 6: Ascension. By now your meeting has happened and you've wowed them in person. You've likely told them that you'll be sending over a quote or proposal for them to accept to move into a business relationship, right?

Believe it or not, that proposal and quote is still a part of your email marketing. The timing that you send this out and the tool that you send this out with will all help you to create an experience that makes it that much easier to ascend into an actual customer relationship with you.

Let's look at some good practices as they relate to sending your proposals and quotes.

Best Practices for sending proposals and quotes:

1) Send it in the time frame that you outlined in your meeting. This matters. If possible, send it sooner. Under-promise and over-

deliver. This simple business principle can take you a long way. If you've stated that your turn-around time for your proposal is seventy-two hours, shoot for forty-eight. It always makes a statement when you over-deliver.

2) Use a system (popularly called a Customer Relationship Manager or CRM; there are plenty to choose from) that will allow the lead to accept the terms, sign a contract if applicable, and pay your fees all in one swoop. This minimizes the need to go back and forth through several administrative emails at this point and makes for a better customer experience. You'll also want to ensure you'll be able to see when the proposal has been viewed, clicked, or un-opened because some follow-up may be needed if your leads don't automatically ascend.

Once your lead has ascended and become a customer, they are now in a paid relationship with you. Your emails from this point until the completion of the project become administrative and will pick up from a marketing prospective once the project is complete. At that point, your client is now ready to move into the next step of the journey, which is the advocacy step of the journey.

Let's look at what emails should be included at this phase of the journey.

Step 7: Advocacy. In the advocacy stage of the customer journey, you are now asking your clients to share their opinion about the relationship you've had so far. If the project is complete, you're asking them to give a testimonial about their experience.

If you're using email at this stage, you want to give instructions for what to include in their testimonials.

Remember that since these testimonials are going to be actively used to help you sell your services in the future, you want your testimonial request to include some specific things to ensure they can be used as selling tools, not just good praise for your website.

Things to ask in your testimonial request email:

1) Ask your client to highlight what they loved about working with you.
2) Ask your client to highlight how they felt during the process.
3) Finally, ask your client to highlight how they feel now that the project is complete.

By asking these three questions of your client, it allows you not only to collect feedback on how to improve, but it also helps you to create a perfect testimonial to share with other prospective clients that will give them insight into what to expect from their own personal experience from you.

Using your client's words helps you to craft a perfect testimonial, even if they don't know how to express what they've experienced in words and gives you client perspectives that will sell for you.

When you share these experiences through your website, presentations, and social media, it will make filling your pipeline that much easier and your emails won't have to work as hard.

It works like magic.

The final step of the journey is the promotion step of the journey. Let's look at what emails can be sent in this stage to help your current clients become promoters of your business.

Step 8: Promotion. This step of the journey is where you want to ask for referrals! This is the last step of the journey before you transition your clients into newsletter recipients to put them back into the beginning of the journey with you.

It's a simple step that I usually send out as a confirmation email once a person has finished my testimonial request.

By now you've seen an example of a few confirmation emails, but allow me to highlight the goal of this confirmation email and what it should accomplish.

Referral Request Email. This email should be sent out as a confirmation of receipt of the customer's testimonial or "feedback." Your email should accomplish the following:

1) Confirm that you've received the feedback given.
2) Thank them for being a great customer.
3) Ask them if there is anyone that they think could benefit from receiving the level of service that they received and if so send them to a form to complete with name, phone number and email.
4) Let them know that you'll be keeping in touch through (weekly, monthly, etc.) newsletters.
5) Give them instructions to make sure you stay connected online at your social platform of choice.

By doing this, you've taken the pressure from asking for a referral, and you've also put yourself in a position to stay connected online. Now, once they see a post of yours, they will automatically share their good experience giving you social proof, again making it easier to build your pipeline.

By now you understand that email marketing is not just about your newsletters, and it's not just a selling tool.

By now you should understand just how effective a few emails can be in driving actual revenue for your business, and how, if used properly, they can keep your sales pipeline full of new prospects, making it easier for you to sell more of your design services.

Pay special attention to the fact that understanding the customer journey and how email plays a role is a crucial part to setting up your initial email marketing system. This system can be set up once and replicated in several different scenarios.

Email marketing is still a very effective tool to closing sales, and it doesn't need to be a difficult process to implement.

It's my hope that you have a much clearer understanding of how to get started with email marketing in your design business, and by implementing this process, you can see much better results from your efforts.

Don't forget to download your FREE workbook to help you complete this chapter.

Download it here: www.kaewhitaker.com/email-workbook

Before I sing Kae's praises, I must say, if you are a brand-new business (and I mean brand-new), a digital marketing plan is not the first thing to tackle. I want you to know and understand the client journey and the basics of email sequencing, but you have some work to do before creating a digital marketing strategy if you are truly one of my #babydesigners.

The first step is to have your brand identified, your logo created, your website developed and launched, a small portfolio of work showcased, some blog content displayed, and a lead magnet created. With these in place, you are ready to create your digital marketing plan.

If you are ready, then download Kae's workbook and dive right in. With her tools and advice, you can choose to either do it yourself, you can purchase Kae's online courses for a guided process, or, like me, you can now hire it out entirely, with Kae or someone else. By hire out, remember the example of designing a home. It requires clear direction from the client to the professional, it requires consistent communication between the client and the professional and it requires the client's trust in the professional to do what they do. Just as with a design project, you can expect the process to include weekly phone calls, it definitely should include scheduled monthly meetings, and it likely includes dozens of emails in between all making sure the messaging and the materials are always on point. It also means that while the firm is executing the big things, you are the voice answering the messages and the emails that the marketing is creating in your in box and in social media. Hired out definitely does not mean checked out.

If you are ready to get started in digital marketing, one area Kae didn't go into in great detail is the creation of the lead magnet itself. This is the free gift you will give someone in exchange for their precious email address. Creating a successful lead magnet is worthy of an entire chapter itself. (Hint: look for that in my third book). In the meantime, to complement Kae's information, refer to these podcast episodes for some insights on lead magnets:

- *Episodes #259 and 274. Kae walks us through a typical email sequence, including examples of the types of calls to action you could create.*
- *Episode #1. A discussion about lead magnets must include Heather McManus. Heather created a thirty-day video series for prospective clients way back in 2015! She was a pioneer in the design industry regarding digital marketing.*
- *Episode #209 Sam Henderson and Leslie Carothers of Savour Partnership discuss how and why you must build your email list if you own a business in this digital age.*

The big take-away: It is imperative to understand what your client's needs are so you can identify the solutions and then provide them through your email marketing in the proper timeline.

- LN

About the Author

Kae Whitaker is the owner and CEO of Kae Whitaker Solutions. With over ten years of experience in retail sales and marketing development, Kae now focuses on helping small businesses build automated marketing systems that help to decrease their workload and increase their profits.

Kae has appeared on LuAnn's podcast five times, on episodes 26, 66, 114, 259, and 274:

https://luannnigara.com/26-kae-whitaker-branding-your-business-finally-i-understand-it/

https://luannnigara.com/66-kae-whitaker-how-to-hire-and-train-interns/

https://luannnigara.com/114-power-talk-friday-kae-whitaker-how-to-make-the-most-of-your-year-end-business-review/

https://luannnigara.com/259-kae-whitaker-get-new-clients-with-the-right-email-sequence/

https://luannnigara.com/274-power-talk-friday-kae-whitaker-part-2-of-email-marketing-for-your-interior-design-firm/

CHAPTER 12

Stacey Brown Randall

I n this chapter, we are going to look at our numbers again. However, where Michele Williams talked to us about our financial numbers, Stacey talks to us about our sales numbers. More specifically, she describes how to track where our clients actually come from.

The true origin of the phrase "what gets measured gets done" is debated. Some say it was coined by the renowned American management consultant Peter Drucker, while others report it was Georg Joachim Rheticus, an Austrian mathematician and astronomer from the 1500s. Here's what I know. I heard it for the first time when Sandra Funk of House of Funk said to me during her podcast interview, "Lu, what gets tracked gets done." Ever since then, experts like Stacey continue to tell us the same thing.

Successful people set goals, track them, analyze the results, make adjustments, and repeat. Measuring both our client base and how they found us is no different. When you know how your past and current clients have found you, you can strategize to attract more from the same resources. Thankfully, Stacey has the system for helping us do exactly this.

- LN

Leveraging Referrals to Grow Your Firm
By Stacey Brown Randall

As a business owner, you have undoubtedly heard that you need to "know your numbers." It is a necessity for all businesses and sound business advice. However, we need to know a few key business numbers beyond just knowing our revenue, expense, profit, and the amount to set aside for taxes. Those often-overlooked, important numbers are your business growth numbers, and I'm not just talking about how many clients you have.

When we break down our business growth numbers, we uncover some powerful data that, when used correctly, allows us to make better business decisions. Those business growth numbers include:

- The number of prospects in your pipeline
- The sources of your clients and prospects
- Your overall close ratio and your close ratio by source
- The number of referral sources and category breakdown

I know that looks like a lot of numbers to keep up with, but by applying simple monthly tracking, you can put your finger on the pulse of how your business growth is performing. A simple spreadsheet is an easy way to build a monthly tracking dashboard. Your project management or CRM software may also be able to provide this data to you as well.

But why is this information so valuable for our businesses? This data informs the actions we should be taking to grow our business. As business owners, we will always find more to do, missed opportunities and a lack of resources and capacity...if we allow it. Being crystal clear on how your business grows allows you to prioritize how you will spend your time. By knowing what is working and what is not working, you can drop activities that are not adding to your growth and spend more targeted time on the activities that are working or should be working.

Let's look at each of the data points in detail following the process I use with my clients. The goal of this process is to provide you with the ability to make actionable decisions in your business right now.

The Number of Prospects in Your Pipeline

I once asked an interior designer about her pipeline and she asked me if I said "piping." First, I was impressed that I knew what "piping" was, but I clarified and asked about her sales or prospect pipeline. That was when I was met with a blank stare.

After a momentary pause, she did say that she had a few proposals out and a meeting coming up with a potential new client. "Was that what I was asking about?" she wanted to know. Yes, but the goal of a clearly identified pipeline with metrics you track is knowing what the next few months or even year looks like in terms of bringing on potential new clients and revenue.

A pipeline is like a funnel (see Figure 1). Prospects enter at the top when they become aware of your business, work their way through the buyer's journey, and with luck—a portion of them—exit the funnel as a new client.

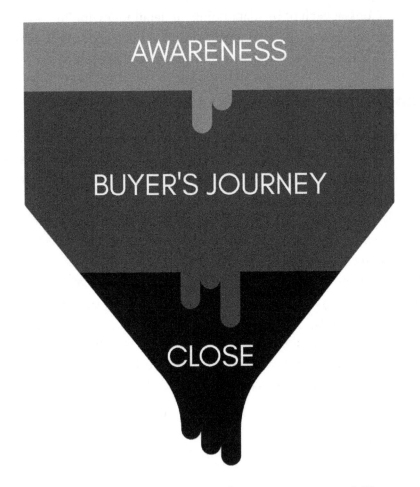

[Image copyright: © 2018 | Stacey Brown Randall]

Using the funnel image above, notice the three stages of the pipeline: the awareness stage, the buyer's journey stage, and the close stage. Depending on how your sales process works, there may be additional steps within each stage. Your buyer's journey may include a few meetings and a proposal before someone says yes or no to working with you, in other words, moving to the final stage (the close stage). Having a handle on your pipeline means being clear on a few points.

1. Being clear on where your prospects come from—how they landed in your pipeline to begin with;
2. How many prospects are in the pipeline at any given time; and
3. Which stage they occupy in the pipeline process.

All stages are critical for the pipeline to work, but if nothing is going into the top of the funnel, then the rest is pointless. Being clear on the number of prospects in your pipeline starts with identifying how prospects enter your funnel. Prospects enter your funnel when they become aware of your business through a source, often called an activity. Activities could be meeting you at a networking event, seeing your ad in a magazine, being referred to you, doing a Google search, finding you on Houzz, and many more.

The Three Plans That Fill Your Pipeline

These individual activities—networking, ads, Houzz, referrals—each belong within one of three plans that make up your overall sales or business development strategy. Those three plans are the prospecting plan, the marketing/branding plan, and the referral plan. Different activities fit within each plan. These three plans are needed in every business, whether you are starting out, sustaining your growth, or trying to get to the next level of growth.

Each of the three plans comprises activities you do to bring prospects into your sales pipeline. Here is a breakdown of each plan as defined by some of the plans' activities, although please note that this does not represent an exhaustive list of activities.

Prospecting Plan

- Attending networking events
- Cold calling
- Joining a leads group

- Cold emailing
- One-on-one networking (coffee, lunch, etc.)
- Buying leads
- Attending trade shows
- Joining associations or membership groups

Marketing/Branding Plan

- Advertising
- Public relations
- Website
- Content marketing
- SEO (search engine optimization)
- Speaking engagements
- Social media marketing

Referral Plan

The referral plan is different because there aren't individual activities you do, as with the prospecting or marketing plan. The referral plan is a process you follow to generate referrals without asking. We'll dive into this plan with our final metric below.

The goal is to build out your overall sales plan with activities or sources from each of the three plans. However, to know which activities to pick, you need to have a handle on what sources are currently working (or are the sources you want to be working) to deliver prospects and eventually clients into your business. This brings us to the next metric we need to have a handle on.

Your Client and Prospect Sources

One of my favorite questions to ask my students in my "Growth By Referrals" program is, "Do you know where your clients come from?" It is a pretty easy question to answer if you have only been in business one to two years, but it becomes more difficult to answer the longer you have been in business, especially if you are not consistently tracking how your clients heard about you or found you.

Stop for a minute and let me ask you the same question, regardless of how long you have owned your interior design firm: do you know based on data, not anecdotal evidence or your memory, where your clients come from? And more specifically where your prospects come from?

With correct tracking of all of your prospects, both those who became clients and those who did not, you can uncover which of your activities are actually working to deliver potential new clients. Why this is so critical is because having a strong grasp on the activities that are working allows you to protect your time from the activities that aren't working. Moreover, this information allows you to know where you need to dedicate more time if you want to increase prospects coming from an individual source.

This was the "a-ha" moment I had after my first business, a human resources consulting firm, failed. I took some time to look into the details of what worked and didn't work with that business. What I discovered was that I never took time to create a sales strategy or plan based on what was working and what was not working. I was just running around, trying to bring in new business in multiple ways—so many ways—and never stopped to hone in on what was actually working.

When I did spend that time unpacking what worked and didn't, albeit too late, I noticed two important trends. One, I generated a good portion of my business through speaking engagements and two, I didn't receive any referrals. That's right, not one.

When I think back to all the time spent—time lost—on attending all of those networking events, one-on-one coffees, publishing articles, white papers ... it makes my head spin. My guess is that after you complete this exercise you might have your head-spinning moment too. Your head-spinning moment might be considering all that money you've spent on home shows, leads or networking groups, sponsorships of events, printed or online advertisements, and more.

Had I taken some time to do the following exercise, I would have identified what was actually working and what was not working. In addition, I would have identified activities or sources that I wanted to develop, such as generating referrals.

Here is what I want you to do.

The Identification Process

First, sit down with a list of your clients; go back as many years back as you can. Looking back two or three years will give you good data, but if you have been in business for, say, ten years, then go back at least five years. Try to go back at least half as many years as you have been in business, depending on length. If you have been in business only one to three years, capture every year worth of data.

If you want a gold star, go back for each year you have been in business. I have had students in my "Growth By Referrals" program who have been in business for ten or fifteen years take the time to pull as much of their client data as possible. I'm sure you can too. Keep in mind, you may be able to pull this information from a CRM tool (client relationship management tool) or do it the old-fashioned way with pen and paper.

Consider this activity a little time spent walking down memory lane.

Starting with clients is always easiest, because it is a list that you can readily pull or have access to since you should have some client data, possibly in a folder, on the work you did with them. With luck, within that data is a notation of how they heard about you. You may get lucky and realize that within your design CRM you captured this information for your clients and all you need to do is pull the list by running a report.

An additional step you can take that will make this data richer and tell a more complete picture is to include prospects you received through any source but who didn't become clients. Why is this important? Because you won't "close" every prospect you work with, but that doesn't mean the source, the activity, doesn't work in terms of generating the prospect. I would venture to say no business owner has a 100 percent close ratio on every prospect they talk to, so we all have prospects we need to account for.

I do recognize that this information, the sources of the prospects who didn't become a client, is harder to capture than just creating a list of clients. Your clients are your clients; of course you know them or know how to pull the information to create the list. But with a prospect, you might have only met them once. Nevertheless, if you can recreate this list of prospects, your data of prospect sources will be stronger and richer.

One tip on how to recreate this prospect list is to do a review of your calendar and make a list of the prospects you have met with. (I color code my prospect meetings in dark green, so it makes it easier to "see" all my prospect meetings when I am skimming my calendar.) Once you have the prospects written down, you can check your emails or files by searching for the prospect's name to see if you captured any information on how they heard about you, found you, or you found them.

When we take the time to create this list of sources from where our clients and our prospects come from, we can leverage important data to make sound and solid decisions for our business.

Once you have your list of sources, captured as where your clients and prospects came from, you can start to identify what is working and what is not. Do a majority of clients come through a handful of referral sources? Or do a number come from a volunteer committee you serve on? Are they responding to your ads or the content you post on social media sites? Are you meeting some of your prospects at the yearly home show? Do many of your clients eventually become repeat clients? Yes, this counts as a source.

Did you notice that you spend thousands and thousands of dollars on ads and that barely register as a source sending you prospects and clients? What about the membership fees you spend on Houzz? Is this outlay working in a way that meets the return on investment that you want? Have you been a member of that networking group for four years that doesn't account for any of your clients? Do you really want to receive more referrals, but you realized you receive barely any?

This is just a good exercise on understanding your business on a whole new level.

Uncovering Gaps

This exercise might uncover a few gaps in the operation of your design firm. I want you to be on the lookout for three in particular.

1. You might realize you haven't been capturing the source information, so you cannot complete the exercise. While a bummer, it is not the end of the world, unless you don't change a critical process in your business. You need to start tracking where your business comes from. Start today by adding a "how did you hear about us?" question to your client intake form, adding the question to your online inquiry form, and training your staff to ask the questions when they take that initial call. If the question is there, do not stand for the practice of skipping it. Whatever you do, just make sure you are capturing the information and keeping it in one place where you can access it when you need it.

2. You may also realize that you aren't clear on which sources work better than others because you haven't identified your overall closing ratio along with the closing ratio by source, and you aren't using that information to inform decisions you should be making.

3. You will be able to identify if your business is taking advantage of the easiest way to grow, which is through referrals that you don't ask for.

Let's unpack your closing ratio first.

Your Overall Close Ratio and Close Ratio by Source

I've noticed when I start talking about close ratio, sometimes I can see eyes start to glaze over. (But not yours, right?) I know that sometimes our eyes glaze over because, honestly, we don't know what it means and sometimes because it just sounds boring. I get it. It is not the most exciting part of running a business. But understanding these ratios is important so we know how to use our time.

Your close ratio is a simple formula which is based on how well you close business. For example, if in a year I had one hundred prospects that considered doing business with me and I turned sixty-two of them into clients, then I would have an overall closing ratio of approximately sixty percent. Now for the best overall closing ratio you need to average your closing ratio over a few years but even one year will provide you with a pretty good indication. The formula works like this:

$$\text{(number of prospects x number of closed clients)} / \text{number of prospects} = \% \text{ closing ratio}$$

Your closing ratio is important because you can reverse engineer how many prospects you need to reach your overall client goal for each year.

If I know I want fifty clients in a year and my closing ratio is fifty percent, then my goal of the number of prospects that I need to be in front of is one hundred. I can then formulate a plan to work towards hitting my goal of one hundred prospects brought into my pipeline, my funnel. Your sales plan is completely ineffective if it doesn't include the actions you are going to take to work each activity so that you can generate the number of prospects needed.

Taking the concept of your close ratio a step further, this process really reveals gold in your business when you can identify the closing ratio by individual sources.

For example, I know my close ratio is significantly higher when a prospect is referred to me than when the prospect finds me through an internet search and lands on my website to download a resource. Here is how the formula works for individual sources.

If I receive ten prospects from referrals (the source) and I close or turn eight of them into clients, then I have a closing ratio of eighty percent with referred prospects. If in a given year, I receive twenty prospects from Houzz and I close five of them, then I know my close ratio with Houzz is twenty-five percent.

Once you have pulled your list of clients and prospects by sources, you can then determine your closing ratio overall and your closing ratio by individual sources. This will take a little work and a calculator. However, this will allow you to plan your sales activities along with the actions to take to make your numbers a reality.

Now let's unpack the other gap you may have identified by completing the activity of knowing the sources of your prospects and clients … which is identifying if your business is taking advantage of the easiest way to grow, through referrals.

Understanding Referrals and Your Referral Sources

The holy grail of how to grow your business with less effort, more ease, and in the most authentic way is to generate referrals: specifically, referrals without asking. A referral is when you're connected with a potential new client by someone (the referral source) and the referral source indicates that the potential new client expressed a need (problem, pain point) they know you can help them solve.

Referrals are the most powerful source of generating clients for a few key reasons. You don't have to go looking for that client; they drop in your lap (or your email inbox); they are less price sensitive because they value you based on what someone else tells them about you; and they are quicker to close because they trust you before meeting with you.

How is this possible? Because of the transfer of trust—the real currency in business—between the person referring you (whom I call the referral source) and the prospect.

It works like this. Once a referral source helps someone (your soon-to-be prospect) identify a need they would like to fix or a pain point or problem in their business they want to solve, they have put the prospect in a position to acknowledge that they do have a problem to solve. Now the prospect has the mindset of wanting to know how to fix the problem. At that moment, the prospect is in a place to want a recommendation on how to solve their particular problem, which your referral source can provide by referring you as the solution provider they trust.

Sometimes the referral source doesn't have to identify the need in the prospect—like it is time to remodel the kitchen, something the prospect has been thinking about since they moved in—but when it is finally time to remodel the kitchen, the will seek out someone they trust to help them decide whom to use to remodel the kitchen. They ask someone they trust for a recommendation. When the referral source connects the prospect to you, the trust the referral source has for you is transferred to the prospect. This transfer of trust between the referral source and the prospect is the critical ingredient in a referral and is not something the other sources like advertising, direct mail, or cold calling can produce in the prospect. This critical piece of trust is what makes a referral a referral.

Trust cannot be artificially created, and you cannot buy it. It must be developed and nurtured. So, when the referral source tells their friend, family member, or colleague that you are the right designer to turn their 1960-style ranch into a modern masterpiece, the prospect trusts that advice, because they trust the person recommending you as the solution.

The Problem with Referrals

The problem with referrals today though is that you have probably been taught or heard that to generate referrals you must ask for them. If you believed you had to ask for referrals and that makes you uncomfortable, you probably just didn't ask for them. This means that you haven't taken the time to create a dedicated process to generate referrals because you left it up to chance. Many interior designers, or, heck, many business owners in general, are in your place. You aren't alone.

The fact is that, for decades we have been taught to ask for referrals. It was effectively the only way to do it, or so said the experts. Luckily, that advice is just not true.

The third plan every business needs is a referral-generating plan. It is the third ingredient in your sales strategy. This is the final piece of business numbers you need to know ... the number of referral sources you have and the category they fall into.

Once you complete the activity of understanding your sources you will know if your business is fueled by referrals or not. A business fueled by referrals receives referrals on a consistent basis from a dedicated group of referral sources that you nurture every year. The list of referral sources is fluid and one you continue to cultivate.

For the final metric, you will need a number of referral sources that you can confirm who they are by name, and you can determine their category breakdown. There are two categories of referral sources ... a client (existing or current) or a Center of Influence (COI). A Center of Influence is a subset of your network who knows what you do, who doesn't do what you do (so you have no competitive overlap with them), and who comes across your ideal client. The reason to know if they are a client versus a COI is that some of the touch points you do are different for a client than a COI.

Let's look at a few examples of COIs so you can start to determine who your COIs may be. For a high-end designer, a COI could be a luxury homebuilder or an architect. For a designer that focuses on remodels, realtors or remodeling companies could be good COIs.

Now don't worry if you don't feel like you have a healthy number of referral sources, you can always develop a referral plan for your business; you just need to know what to do.

Understanding the Referral Plan

What makes the referral plan different from the other plans is that the referral plan doesn't have individual, stand-alone activities as in the prospecting or marketing plans. The referral plan is a process you follow made up of memorable and meaningful touch points while planting referral seeds, so you can generate referrals without asking. In effect, to build your referral plan you need to:

- Identify who are your referral sources (referral source = people who refer you)
- Build relationships with referral sources
- Know how to plant referral seeds so you never ask for referrals
- Follow a process to turn "soon-to-be" referral sources into referral sources

Knowing who your referral sources are is important because it determines how much work you need to do if you want to build consistent and sustainable referral generation in your business.

The ultimate goal for following the process above for building a referral plan is to increase referrals as the largest source for how prospects fill your funnel. When referrals are the largest percentage of prospects in our pipeline, we can shift how we spend our time and grow our business in the easiest way possible.

The business growth numbers of knowing the prospects in your pipeline, the sources of your clients and prospects, your close ratios, and the number of referral sources allow you to be in control of your business and make better decisions on how you want to grow your business, on your terms. While we don't control the outcome of every action we take—we can't make a prospect become a client—we do control our actions and knowing your business growth numbers is one action that is within your grasp. Take the action today to "know your numbers."

Gathering this information is the start of intentionally maximizing your current client base for building your business. If you are not already recording how each of your prospective clients has learned about you (not merely counting sold clients, but instead every single inquiry), no matter how many years you are in business, please start now. No excuses. You will use this information to determine, among other things, where you should advertise and the budget you should allot each initiative. Then at the end of each year, you will again analyze the results so that you can evaluate the effectiveness of the advertising decisions you made.

You have heard me say it on the show many times, our business at Window Works is now largely referral based, hovering over sixty percent. My personal sales are closer to 75 percent referral based. High referral rates lead to high close rates, as well as high gross profit margins; both lead to healthy, profitable numbers.

How do I know this?

We do ask every single person that calls us, whether they make a shop at home appointment or not. We have done this from day one going back to when we recorded it in a notebook, long before personal computers were a thing.

Now, thankfully, the answers get entered into our CRM under their client profile along with their name, address, email address, and interests. We use some two dozen codes to indicate the referral source. Here are some examples:

- *prv: the person themselves is a previous customer*
- *prv cus: the person calling was referred by someone who was a customer*
- *rea: referral from realtor*
- *ref des: referral from designer*
- *des trade: designer client*
- *dm hh: direct mail - House & Home magazine*
- *ref pod: referral from podcast!*

Each code lets us know at a glance how this prospect came to us. This is helpful not only at year end, but it is also helpful in real time for the salesperson going into the home. I realize that as designers, you are not likely to go on thirty, forty, or fifty new appointments each month, so it is much easier for you to "know" your clients and their details. However, as you grow your business over the next five years, ten years, and longer, you will be grateful you collected this information.

Seasoned business owners also know that the most efficient, economical way to do build your pipeline is through referrals. You have been told to ask the client for a referral at the end of every project:

"I'm so happy you love what we did for you here. Do you know any friends that would like their entire home redesigned?"

Ugh. I know. I don't do that either.

You'll be glad to learn Stacey debunks this theory of flat out asking for referrals. For more information on the next step (after tracking and understanding your sales numbers) which is how to actually get more referrals through relationship building rather than asking for them tune in to Stacey's podcast: Roadmap to Grow Your Business and be sure to get her book too.

Stacey's chapter, combined with her podcast and her book, are powerful tools to help you grow your client base and grow your profits.

- LN

About the Author

Stacey Brown Randall is a contrarian on how to generate referrals. Through her Growth by Referrals program, she provides a roadmap for small business owners and solopreneurs to generate referrals without asking. She is the author of *Generating Business Referrals ... Without Asking* and host of the *Roadmap to Grow Your Business* podcast. Stacey received her master's in organizational communication and is married with three kids. Find her at **StaceyBrownRandall.com**.

Stacey has appeared on LuAnn's podcast twice, on episodes 69 and 93:

https://luannnigara.com/69-power-talk-friday-stacey-brown-randall-take-control-of-your-business-employee-management/

https://luannnigara.com/93-power-talk-friday-stacey-brown-randall-how-to-create-an-awesome-client-experience/

Conclusion

Are you ready? Are you ready to run your business the way you know you can? Say, "Yes, yes, I am!"

The thirteen of us have taken our time to share our experiences with you so that your journey can be easier and more intentional than ours has been. Not one of us sprouted as a fully formed business guru. We have each had our failures, as well as the moments when we wondered if we would make it. I promise you that.

Often, I am asked when will I not be afraid to hire someone, to rent a studio, to say no to the wrong client? The answer is never. You will never be completely free from fear. The hard truth is that it always scary to take risks and to put yourself, your reputation, and your business on the line. However, you can learn to evaluate, minimize, and manage that risk.

Consider this: you probably have created dozens, or even hundreds, of beautiful rooms in your career so far. Does that mean you never have to worry about making a design mistake? No. Does it stop you from designing? No. You learn from it, you remember it, and you take steps to do better next time. It's just the same with running your business. It is okay to fail, it is okay to be terrified, it is just plain okay.

It is not okay to be stuck.

Learn how to operate your business with your eyes wide open, commit to learn the parts that are harder for you to understand, and always seek council from those who have achieved success. It is completely within your capability to learn sound business principles so you can make quality assessments that lead to solid decisions.

In my first book, I stated, "I believe, to truly be successful, you must possess the powerful combination of confidence, a plan, and the decision to take action."

Think about these statements:

- Can I be successful if I have confidence and a decision, but no plan? *Maybe … good luck with that. That sounds like a long and painful process to me.*

- Can I be successful if I have a plan and a decision, but no confidence? *Hmm. It strikes me as it is unlikely you will follow through.*

And the saddest of all:

- Can I be successful if I have confidence and a plan, but no decision to act? *Everything, anything, is impossible without a decision to act.*

The Plan

We have created the foundation for you. The twelve chapters in this book contain valuable information which you can refer to again and again. Each chapter touches on something you can use to grow and improve your business. Each chapter gives you a baseline that you can use to make your plan. Need to fill your pipeline? Open Fred Berns' chapter. Struggling to raise your fees? Go to Nancy Ganzekaufer's chapter. Ready to finally get real with your finances? Reread Michele Williams's chapter. This is real-life advice, much of it hard earned by the author, for you to follow so you can grow your interior design business intentionally and systematically.

Confidence

I do hope we have given you a sense of confidence that you can do this. We know it requires tremendous faith in yourself to be self-employed. It requires dedication and commitment every day, every week, every month, every year, year after year after year. Did I just scare you again? I hope not. That is not my intention. My intention is to let you know you are not alone. And to let you know, if you need to, borrow the confidence from us for a while, until you own it yourself. Take confidence in knowing we have used these same strategies in creating our successful businesses. You can trust these lessons will work for you just as they have for us. We have all been where you are. The smart entrepreneur learns from those before them and around them. Be that business owner. Be the business owner who trusts and understands if it has worked for someone else, it will work for me too.

Decide

This is the only one I cannot help you with. You have to own this one. You have to be the one to look in the mirror now. Although you can picture each of us standing by you at that mirror, if you want. In fact, I'd love for you to do just that. The decision, though, that is all you. Take responsibility for your business and tackle each of these areas, one by one.

Many of our colleagues will read this book and have a genuine rush of inspiration. But how many will turn the inspiration into action? Take a moment to look ahead one year, three years, ten years, and thirty years from now. What will you say to yourself in each of these moments?

In one year, I want you to say, "I tackled two really hard systems last year, mastered them, and I have my sights on two more next year".

In three years, I want you to say, "I am running a profitable business because I understand the principles of business and I continue to seek help in areas where I am not as strong."

In ten years, I want you to say, "My business enjoys noticeable success because I continue to set and reach my goals."

In thirty years, I want you to say, "I did this. I created a business I am proud of, a business that has benefitted and touched many lives. I have clients who love where they live and work because of me, I have employees who have grown and prospered because of me. My business matters to me, to my family, and to my community."

You got this. I know it. I have faith in you.

-LN

Made in the
USA
Middletown, DE